FORGED

33 DAYS
TOWARD
FREEDOM

Totus Tuus
PRESS

JASON EVERT | MATT FRADD

For Mary

CONTENTS

Introduction *9*

Welcome to Forged *15*

Preliminary Days

Day 1   What Are You Looking For? *20*

Day 2   Where Are You? *25*

Day 3   Where Is Your Hope? *28*

PART ONE

The Furnace: Purified for Strength

Day 4   Lift Up Your Hearts *37*

Day 5   Know Your Enemy *42*

Day 6   Get to the Roots *46*

Day 7   Identify Your Triggers *52*

Day 8   Renounce Your Affection for Sin *57*

Day 9   Redeem Fatherhood *60*

Day 10 Build Brotherhood *64*

Day 11 Be Absolved *69*

Day 12   Keep Track *74*

Day 13   Guard Your Peace *77*

PART TWO

The Hammer and Anvil: Shaped for a Purpose

Day 14   Struggle with Lust. *83*

Day 15   Flee Idleness *87*

Day 16   Starve Your Lust *91*

Day 17   Manage Withdrawal. *95*

Day 18   Fuel Your Desire *99*

Day 19   Pray for Your Temptations *103*

Day 20   Sacrifice Your Desire to Be Tempted. . . *108*

Day 21   Avoid the Location of Sin *111*

Day 22   Quit Justifying. *115*

Day 23   Consider Counseling *112*

PART THREE

The Grinding Stone: Polished for Perfection

Day 24   Mortify Your Flesh *127*

Day 25   Fast *131*

Day 26   Read Sacred Books *135*

Day 27   Practice Silence *139*

Day 28   Listen to Him *143*

Day 29   Remember Your Guardian Angel *146*

Day 30   Go to St. Joseph *151*

Day 31   Behold Your Mother *155*

Day 32   Be Intensely Eucharistic *159*

Day 33   Live in Freedom *165*

Forged to Fight *168*

Endnotes *173*

Imagine standing before the throne of God on judgment day, where the great saints of ages past, who themselves dealt with preeminent sins in their own day, will say to each other, "We dealt with the trouble of lust in our day, but those 21st century men! These happy few battled the beast up close!"

—Bishop Thomas Olmsted, *Into the Breach*

INTRODUCTION

GOOD MEN DON'T need more reasons why it's wrong to use women—whether it be online, in their imagination, or in reality. What they need are effective strategies to win daily battles and to obtain lasting freedom and victory in the war against lust. For this reason, we created *Forged*. It's not for the perfect man. It's for imperfect ones who still strive for perfection.

When steel is forged, it is heated at temperatures above 2,000 degrees in order for the material to become malleable. A blacksmith then compresses it under extreme pressure or pounds it against an anvil in order to form its shape, before grinding and polishing it to perfection. When it cools, the material is not only more useful as a tool or weapon but is significantly stronger because of how the forging process improves its crystal structure.

In the same manner, the thirty-three days of this program are intentionally demanding. They are formulated to deconstruct you in order that you might be restructured and restored to a new level of interior strength. Although the process will involve discomfort, we encourage you to give it your all.

Saint Thomas Aquinas defined *effeminacy* as the unwillingness of a man to put aside his pleasures in order to pursue what is difficult. When a man becomes accustomed to an excess of pleasure, it becomes difficult for him to endure the lack of it. His inordinate attachment to sensuality, relaxation, and play renders him soft. He becomes too delicate to endure toil.[1] In no era of human history has this been more of a temptation than our own because of the endless stream of pleasurable distractions available online. Therefore, our culture desperately needs men who are willing to battle vigorously against the allurements of an effeminate life.

It is important to note that effeminacy does not mean same-sex attractions. Unfortunately, many men who experience homosexual attractions have been told that they are less manly because of it. But manliness isn't measured by a man's desires. Christian manhood is measured by a man's willingness to conform his life to Jesus Christ crucified, regardless of his attractions. It would be convenient if masculinity could be gauged by the intensity of a man's attraction to women. But that's not how it works. In fact, the men who pride themselves on their sexual conquests of women often tend to be the most effeminate. Regardless of what your attractions may be, we're all in this together.

This battle for sexual integrity is not something that a man wins in thirty-three days. It is a lifelong conflict. It is also not something that a man wins in isolation. For this reason, *brotherhood* is an essential component of this book. In fact, this brief program offers only a foretaste of the deeper progress that will unfold through the fellowship that it creates.

Our first challenge to you is to find a brother (or several) who will undertake this journey with you. Or if you're able, do the program at home as father and son. This invitation is not merely for your sake; it is also for theirs, because one of the marks of authentic friendship is a shared striving for mutual perfection. As Scripture states: "Iron sharpens iron, and one man sharpens another" (Prov 27:17). Therefore, before you begin, find brothers who will join you in the program and stay in daily contact with them, checking in with short conversations and sometimes longer discussions on how it's going. Imagine how many others you can help by having the courage and humility to invite them to join you.

A second key element of this book is *intentionality*. This text is not intended as leisurely bedtime reading or something you try to fit into your daily schedule if time allows. We ask that you set your alarm clock ten minutes early each day for the following thirty-three days, to read the book before beginning your daily routines. Be deliberate in winning the first moment of each day. This victory begins tonight when you set your alarm.

The third and final key is *consistent perseverance*. These exercises are not a sprint. Pace yourself and don't skip ahead. Aim to stay on track, regardless of any setbacks you may experience.

The program begins with three introductory days, followed by three ten-day courses. Just as the process of forging involves heat, pressure, and polishing, the three parts of this program will correspond to this model of transformation. At first, intense heat is applied in order to purify and strengthen the metal. Then, the material is pounded and shaped to be formed for its purpose. Then, it is polished for perfection.

Each day will include a variety of unique strategies and challenges. Whether you struggle with purity online, with yourself, or with another person, these exercises are intended to lead you further down the path of self-mastery, gradually replacing old vices with new virtues and habits. Each day offers you a unique weapon that you can add to your arsenal. When the thirty-three days are completed, you will be well equipped for the battles ahead.

However, the purpose of this book is not simply to build up your defenses. Sobriety from lustful behavior is not the ultimate goal. True sexual healing enables a man to resist the counterfeit of lust, but more importantly it liberates him to make a gift of himself in love. Self-giving is impossible without self-mastery.

To begin our journey together, text the word "Forged" to 66866 (or go to chastity.com/forged). When you do this, for the next thirty-three days we will send you a short, three-minute video every day from different men and women, to accompany you on the way. You're not alone in this journey, and the advice you'll receive through these daily videos will offer you tremendous inspiration and formation. Know that all of us are praying for you.

—Jason Evert

WELCOME TO FORGED

YOU HAVE BEEN born into a pornified culture. That wasn't your fault. You didn't ask for that. Your first exposure to pornography—do you remember it?—that probably wasn't your fault either. The fact that you liked what you saw, that you wanted to see more, that's not just understandable but natural. You have been made by God to desire love, touch, and intimacy. If you didn't find those images at least slightly intriguing, that would be odd.

Having said that, you now have a very important decision to make. Will you let yourself be carried along mindlessly by this pornified culture? Or will you fight against it and your vices to be a better person? Will you waste time blaming everything else (it's my dad's fault; the porn industry's fault; the fact that I was always picked last in soccer!), or will you have the courage to look yourself squarely in the eye and realize—not just realize, but decide— that *you* need to change?

The fact that you're reading this book tells me that you do have that courage, and for that I commend you. *Seriously*, good for you! Many people lack that courage.

The porn industry would have us believe that pornography is a healthy form of entertainment for well-rounded adults. You and I know differently. We know that porn is, to be frank, lame. There's nothing "mature" about it. It is a drearily predictable means of becoming a narrow-minded and, well, uninteresting individual. This is always the case with those immersed in sin. They're not, contrary to what the world would have us believe, open minded and fully alive, they're dull. It is the saints who are free!

Whether you've been struggling with lust on a daily basis for years now, or whether it's only recently become an issue, I want you to know something: victory from this stuff is possible. But please don't misunderstand me, victory isn't a destination. You won't wake up after having read this book, and cry, "Victory!" Well, you might, but it won't be because you have attained it once and for all. No, victory over lust is one day at a time, a daily—and in some cases hourly—decision.

I was once hooked on porn, would look at it every day. It always left me disappointed and empty, but by God's grace, good friends, accountability, and patient perseverance, I can attest to the fact that you don't need to live in slavery.

But perhaps porn isn't your struggle. Maybe it's your imagination, impurity when you're alone, or when you're with a woman. Maybe you experience same-sex attractions and also want to grow in purity. No matter what the case may be, we're all in this together and this book has been created for you, to help you grow in true freedom.

Be of good cheer! This is a new day for you. It's going to be difficult, but isn't that true of anything worthwhile? As Pope Benedict XVI once said, "The world promises you comfort, but you weren't made for comfort, you were made for greatness."

Are you ready? Let's do this!

—Matt Fradd

PRELIMINARY DAYS

DAY 1

WHAT ARE YOU LOOKING FOR?

AS YOU BEGIN this thirty-three-day journey toward freedom, this is the first question we'd like you to ask yourself. What brings you here? Are you reading this because a friend invited you to? Did you choose this on your own because you've noticed that lust for your girlfriend seems to be eroding the love in your relationship? Have you been trying to break free from porn or masturbation, only to fall repeatedly into the same old habits? Does your imagination seem to be overrun with thoughts that you would be mortified for anyone to know? Or, perhaps you're married and have noticed that lust has been contaminating your marriage. Are you feeling frustrated, tired, shameful, or guilty? Regardless of where you're at, you're not alone.

If you've been told that your sexual desires are the problem, we want to tell you that this is a lie. The goal of this program is not to extinguish desire or to offer you a month's worth of coping mechanisms to avoid shameful feelings. God branded within you an unquenchable desire to be united to what is beautiful. It's useless to fight this craving. What's needed is *not* a systematic formula to repress this urge. What's needed is for the ache itself to be set ablaze with God's love. But what does that look like, and how is it possible?

Consider what C. S. Lewis said in his sermon, *The Weight of Glory:*

> It would seem that Our Lord finds our desires not too strong, but too weak. We are half-hearted creatures, fooling about with drink and sex and ambition when infinite joy is offered us, like an ignorant child who wants to go on making mud pies in a slum because he cannot imagine what is meant by the offer of a holiday at the sea. We are far too easily pleased.[2]

In other words, God planted into every soul a thirst that He longs to satisfy beyond anything we can ask or imagine. However, as C. S. Lewis adds, most of human history has been "the long terrible story of man trying to find something other than God which will make him happy."[3]

Or as another man said, "The young man who rings the bell at the brothel is unconsciously looking for God."[4] It's a bit jarring to think that a man hiring a prostitute is looking for Jesus. If he wanted Jesus, he could have just put on a nice outfit and gone to church, right?

The idea of swapping a visible and tangible source of pleasure for an invisible and intangible God seems unappealing. But what if pleasure and purity aren't enemies? What if human sexuality was invented by the same God who inspired the Psalmist to write, "in thy presence there is fullness of joy, in thy right hand are pleasures for evermore" (Ps 16:11)? What if God isn't stingy after all? What if we're the ones who have been stingy with Him? If we trusted Him not only with our souls, but also with our bodies, what would happen?

The reason why C. S. Lewis mentioned the "terrible" story of man is because nothing other than God ultimately works. We may get momentary pleasure from lust, but not joy. In the words of St. Josemaría Escrivá, "When you have sought the company of a sensual satisfaction, what loneliness afterward!"[5] If this has been true for you, know that you're not alone. The authors of this book and the speakers you'll see in your daily videos have all tasted this aloneness.

Beginning today, make a new effort to not seek what cannot satisfy, but turn instead to Him who can.

ACTION

Ancient cisterns were man-made reservoirs built underground in arid regions to retain rainwater. Unlike wells, which draw upon flowing waters deep underground, a cistern is only as useful as its water-proof lining. If the cistern is broken, then no matter how much water is poured into it, it will be useless for quenching one's thirst. For this reason, when Israel turned away from God, the Lord said, "For my people have committed two evils: they have forsaken me, the fountain of living waters, and hewed out cisterns for themselves, broken cisterns that can hold no water" (Jer. 2:13). When we turn to lust in order to quench our thirst for love, we deprive ourselves of what can bring true satisfaction. We carve out broken cisterns hoping that they will gratify us.

Today, we want to invite you to take an honest inventory of your interior life. First, take a look at what the "broken cistern" in your life may be when it comes to your sexuality. Is it escaping into fantasy or indulging in lustful thoughts? An impure relationship with a woman? Porn? Masturbation?

But don't stop there. Don't dwell on the brokenness of the cistern. What's the thirst that sends you there? What are you looking for? Is it relief? Is it release? Is it companionship? Is it the desire to know another or be known deeply? Is it a longing to see or to be seen? Have you found solace by withdrawing into the habit? Don't rush through these questions. Reread them one at a time slowly and seek the answers.

The insights you gain from each exercise in this book will be directly proportional to the amount of effort you put into them. Simply reading the questions and shutting the book will be as beneficial as walking into a gym, looking at the weights, and exiting. Take your time, exert yourself, and do not be afraid to seek the truth. Open your heart, and God will begin to reveal things to you that had been unseen.

DAY 2

WHERE ARE YOU?

WHEN ADAM AND Eve committed the first sin, the first question God asked them was "Where are you?" Since God is all-knowing, He wasn't asking about their location. The deeper question was where they had placed themselves in relation to Him. Adam replied, "I heard the sound of thee in the garden, and I was afraid, because I was naked; and I hid myself" (Gen 3:10).

We often complain that God is difficult to find, while we are the ones who have hidden ourselves from Him because of shame. Perhaps our desire to hide from Him comes from our desire to avoid looking even at ourselves. Today, we invite you to reject the temptation to hide. Take an honest look at who you are and who you wish to be. The purpose of this, as you will see, is not to heap guilt upon you or to focus merely on the negative.

Ask yourself: "What kind of man do I want to be?" Before you answer, don't think "What *should*

I say?" or even "What would *God* want me to say?"
Just be honest.

Also, ask yourself: "How do I want to be remembered when I'm dead? What do I hope will be said
of me in my eulogy?"

Now set down this book for a few minutes and
answer those two questions as honestly as you can.
Seriously. Set down the book.

We'll bet that "the kind of man who's addicted
to lust" is not what you thought of. No matter how
much you may struggle in that area, there's a deeper
current running within you, longing for something
greater. God created you good! Sure, you have your
weaknesses, as all men do. But if you allow God
to look at you, you'll notice that He sees you as a
beloved son, not as a disappointment. Derive your
strength from His glance instead of hiding from it.

ACTION

In the Gospel, Jesus encounters a paralyzed man
who had been lying in the same spot for thirty-eight
years. Jesus asks him a striking question: "Do you
want to be healed?" How does the man respond?
With self-pity and by blaming others: "Sir, I have

no man to put me into the pool when the water is troubled, and while I am going another steps down before me" (John 5:6–7).

Read the full text of John 5:1–17, and then meditate on it. As you do, picture yourself as the paralyzed man. Jesus asks you if you want to be free. What is your reply? Do you desire healing . . . but others prevent you? Do you desire freedom . . . as long as it's easy? Do you desire freedom . . . as long as you can retain a few bad habits? What excuses have you been making—are you *still* making? And most importantly, where do you need healing?

If you truly desire freedom, God wants the same for you. But it will come at a price. "To defend his purity," wrote St. Josemaría Escrivá, "Saint Francis of Assisi rolled in the snow, Saint Benedict threw himself into a thornbush, Saint Bernard plunged into an icy pond . . . You . . . what have *you* done?"[6] He also said, "Don't say, 'That's the way I am—it's my character.' It's your *lack* of character. . . . Be a man!"[7] These words may seem harsh, but sometimes a charitable smack upside the head does more good for a man than gentle words that flatter him. Don't be afraid to ask yourself: "Is it that I couldn't be trying any more to avoid lust, or that I couldn't be trying any less?"

DAY 3

WHERE IS YOUR HOPE?

YESTERDAY, WE ENCOURAGED you to take a deep look at areas of your life that may need healing. Doing this can sometimes leave you feeling discouraged. However weak you may feel, keep in mind the words of St. Paul:

> And to keep me from being too elated by the abundance of revelations, a thorn was given me in the flesh, a messenger of Satan, to harass me, to keep me from being too elated. Three times I besought the Lord about this, that it should leave me; but he said to me, "My grace is sufficient for you, for my power is made perfect in weakness." I will all the more gladly boast of my weaknesses, that the power of Christ may rest upon me. (2 Cor 12:7–9)

We don't know what this "thorn" was, but it's clear that St. Paul's hope was not in himself. His hope was in God alone. Although you may be tempted to focus only on the times you fall, keep in mind that God also keeps track of your victories. He doesn't identify you by your vices or your virtues, so neither should you define yourself by these things. After all, the Christian life is not a contest to win the love of God.

We've all made mistakes. In fact, if Jesus came back tonight, He wouldn't say, "Okay, virgins on the right, nonvirgins on the left!" He would separate us by those fighting for their purity and those who won't. The fact that you're reading this book shows that you are on the right side of the battle. Even if you've made mistakes, you can begin again. You can recommit to chastity and watch your life take on a whole new meaning. Step number one in doing this is rejecting self-reliance and placing all your hope in Him.

ACTION

If purity is above all a gift from God, then our goal ought to be to dispose ourselves to receive this gift from Him. To do this, you need a spiritual plan of life. Just as the world offers you an incessant opportunity to lust, God never ceases to offer the grace needed to love. To access this divine assistance, we invite you to structure your life according to the following plan for the next thirty days. After you implement this plan of life, our hope is that it will become a lifelong habit.

Step One: *Lectio Divina*

For the past three days, hopefully you have set your alarm clock ten minutes early. Reading the book has probably taken up only half of that time. With the rest of your time, pray *Lectio Divina*, which means Divine Reading. To do this, find the daily Mass readings (see chastity.com/forged). Then, find a quiet place where you won't be interrupted and pause to recall that you are in the Holy Presence of God. Consider how He sees you in prayer. Ask Him to make your time of prayer fruitful. Then, read today's Gospel slowly, and pick one word or phrase that struck you. Ponder what God is saying to you through this, and how you can apply it to your upcoming day.

Step Two: Carry a Rosary

Find a rosary, have a priest bless it, put it in your pocket, and keep it there for the next month. That's all. Seriously, that's all we're asking. If you can pray a daily Hail Mary, a decade, or whole rosary, even better! The rosary only takes a quarter of an hour, and if you divide your day into fifteen-minute increments, there are ninety-six of these time slots per day. Give one of them to Our Lady. It can be while you're walking to class, driving to work, or in prayer at church. But if you're not ready for that, okay. All we ask is that you carry one with you for now. (If you don't know how to pray the rosary, you can learn how at chastity.com/forged.) In reference to the rosary, the Virgin Mary once said to St. Padre Pio, "With this weapon you will win."[8] Therefore, arm yourself. Think of the rosary in your pocket as your "concealed carry."

Step Three: Evening Examen

Before you go to bed, carve out a few minutes for night prayer. Contrary to what many people think, an evening examine is not your opportunity to tally up all your failures of the day. Fr. Michael Gaitley suggests you use the acronym B.A.K.E.R. to do this:

B: Blessings. Consider the blessings God gave you today. St. Ignatius taught that this is the

most important of the five points. Spend the
most time on this.

A: Ask. Ask the Holy Spirit to help you recognize
your sins.

K: Kill. Our sins crucified Jesus. Examine your
day and look for places where you turned from
God in your thoughts, words, or deeds, or
omissions.

E: Embrace. Allow God's mercy to embrace you.
Take your time to dwell on this point without
rushing to the next.

R: Resolution. Consider what you gained from
this examination and make resolutions focused
on the next day.

You may want to bookmark this page of the
book, so you can refer back to this acronym until
you have it memorized. If you use the spiritual tools
above and remain disciplined and consistent in this
habit over the next thirty days, God will intervene
in your life in ways that far surpass anything we
could write in a book.

Your morning prayer and evening examination are the bookends of your day. If they are in place, everything between them will be well ordered. Pull one or the other out, and things are likely to get messy. You may be tempted to think "I don't have time to pray." But, if we're honest, we make time for whatever we love, whether it be friends, social media, sports . . . or sin. What we lack isn't time. What we lack is love. We don't have the love to pray. Ask God for this love. And ask Him for purity. After all, purity is not a destination. The destination is heaven. Purity is the daily virtue that helps us get there.

PART ONE

THE FURNACE:
PURIFIED FOR STRENGTH

AS MENTIONED IN the introduction, when steel is placed into a blazing furnace, the heat *softens* the metal so that it can become pliable for the blacksmith, *removes impurities* from the steel, and *strengthens* the object by rearranging its grain structure. This first segment of our program has been crafted for the same purpose. Like steel, the heart of man cannot be shaped and strengthened unless it is first made soft and, thus, open to change.

However, this may require a brutal amount of self-honesty, humility, and vulnerability. It will involve a deep look into one's sexual attitudes, fantasies, beliefs, memories, and habits. Although many of our desires are good and natural, an honest examination will also reveal core lies that must be exposed, unseen wounds in need of healing, and unclean bonds that must be renounced. Without venturing into these dark places and bringing the light of Christ into them, a new structure cannot be built.

If the process of peering deep into your soul feels messy at times, that's okay. It has been said that *most sinners think that they are saints, but true saints know that they are sinners.* It is a sinner's self-awareness that starts him on the path to God. What allows for sainthood is a sinner's honesty about "where they really are" in relationship to Him. But do not be afraid. Your identity is not a porn addict, a guy who keeps messing up with his girlfriend, or a person who can't break the habit of masturbation. Your identity is a son of God. You are loved, and God will complete the good work He began in you (Phil 1:6).

As you progress through this first part of the book, continue with your morning *Lectio Divina* and evening examen. Also, when you put your rosary in your pocket each morning, offer up one Hail Mary, entrusting your day to Our Lady.

DAY 4

LIFT UP YOUR HEARTS

WE KNOW OF a mother who worked in the medical profession and wanted to persuade her son to practice abstinence until marriage. To motivate him to embrace the lifestyle, she showed him several gruesome photographs of sexually transmitted diseases. After the slideshow, he announced to her, "Mom, I now know what I do *not* want to be when I grow up!" "What's that?" she asked. He replied, "I do not want to be a sexually transmitted disease photographer."

Fear motivates no one to be virtuous. The same is true of shame, guilt, and embarrassment. All of these emotions might temporarily dissuade a person from indulging, but they are insufficient catalysts to create lasting change. The temptation to lust is such a powerful drive that there is perhaps only one sufficient remedy for it, and that is our call to love. We must fight desire with desire. As we begin this program with you, we encourage you raise your hearts above motives such as fear and guilt. Why go to the effort of overcoming lustful habits? If you feel called to marriage, do this for love of your bride—even if you haven't met her yet! Think about her when you're tempted to settle for less. Think of how you want your future children to see you. If you think you may have a different calling in life, such as the priesthood, the religious life, or serving God in singleness, you can still sacrifice for the love of others. Although our motives vary, the purest is to live for the glory of God.

No matter what drives you, by entering into this thirty-three-day journey, you're aligning yourself with an army of brothers who are also fighting for a mission greater than themselves. In the words of Pope Benedict XVI ,"That means that in the end I just have to drop the question as to what I get out of it. I have to learn to recognize that it is important to just let myself go. I have to be ready to give myself."[9]

ACTION

One of the challenges of breaking free from lust is that the "rewards" of pleasure seem immediate, whereas any negative consequences seem far removed. But by the time the damage is assessed, the harm has already been done. What if you could move ahead in time, to the place where you hope to be in a decade? If all the habits that are in your life now have not been uprooted and healed, what would that life look like?

Consider the following testimonies given by three women whose husbands viewed porn:

> He is not really with *me*, not really making love to *me* . . . he seems to be thinking about something else or someone else—likely those porn women . . . he is just using me as a warm body.[10]

> Pornography tears at the very thread of a woman and her femininity. My heart was ripped and uprooted . . . It's as if I wasn't enough. Not sexy enough. Not beautiful enough. Not thin enough. Not exciting enough. Women get significance from their relationships with their husbands and when he turns to another for satisfaction it cuts her deeply at the core.[11]

> My husband of a little over one month is in love with pornography. I've tried to speak with him about it before, but I get nervous and flustered and end up nodding to whatever he says.

He does not believe his indulging this desire is cheating or harmful or anything to be ashamed of. He knows I disagree with him, but I doubt he even begins to comprehend how devastating and heartbreaking it is for me. There have already been plenty of nights that he's spent on the computer and doesn't return to share a bed with me at all (he'll fall asleep on the couch or in the guest room). I pray for him and for us every day, but I don't know what else to do. I can already see his relationship with porn damaging other aspects of our marriage, especially in my behavior toward him.[12]

When you read these words, we imagine that your first thought is that you would never want to subject your bride to these feelings of betrayal and insecurity. While some men blame their wives for overreacting and being prudish, a true man upholds the dignity of all women, not just the one he's married to. Our purpose in sharing these stories is not to shame you, but to kindle within you a desire to protect every woman's heart.

These wives aren't the only ones being deprived. Their husbands have also robbed themselves of the ability to be captivated by their brides. Spare your future marriage the suffering, and resolve to do whatever it takes to slay lust in all its forms. What's at stake is love, your family, and your vocation. Therefore, fight for the women in the porn industry. Fight for your bride. Fight for your sisters in humanity. It's not enough to avoid using women. We're called to defend their honor.

The battlefield, however, is not outside us. It's within the heart of every man. This is why the hidden battles are of the greatest importance. That's where the war is won or lost. For this reason, God invites us to be pure in heart. From there, all our actions will flow. Through the redemption of our hearts, we will live out that redemption in our bodies. If you win this, you control the body. If you win this, you win freedom. Therefore, examine your motives today and lift up your heart. Your sacrifices will become a source of joy if they're done for love.

If you feel called to marriage, one way to begin this redemption of our desires is to offer up a prayer right now for your future bride. Don't wait until you meet her to begin loving her. Rather, honor her *all the days of your life.*

DAY 5

KNOW YOUR ENEMY

LET'S MAKE THIS clear from the outset: Sex is not the enemy. The enemy is not your desires, nor is it the women in the porn industry. If anything, the goal of this book is to deepen your appreciation for the gift of sexuality, set your desires ablaze, and *increase* your love for porn stars! However, there is one enemy that doesn't want any of that to happen: Satan.

Some modern thinkers—even religious ones—dismiss his existence and claim that demons are nothing more than literary figures created by ancient writers to personify evil or describe mental illness. However, if this is the case, then the public ministry of Jesus Christ reveals a man utterly detached from reality. In the Gospel of Mark, Jesus is tempted by the devil in the wilderness, and then His first public miracle in that gospel is the exorcism of an unclean spirit—whom He converses with (Mark 1:23–26). That night, he casts out more demons. Do you know what He does the next morning? You guessed it: He casts out more demons. When questioned about his mission, He replied that "no one can enter a strong man's house and plunder his goods, unless he first binds the strong man; then indeed he may plunder his house" (Mark 3:27). Satan is the "strong man" and Jesus has come to bind him, enter his house, and plunder his goods by redeeming humanity.

Jesus Christ came not only to redeem our souls, though. He also came to redeem our bodies and even our desires. Sexuality was never the devil's idea. In fact, it repulses him because of how the life-giving love of a man and woman reflect the creative love of God. God invented sex—it was His idea—and sex is sacred. In fact, the word "sacred" comes from a Latin term that means "holy." When something is sacred it is connected to God and deserves reverence. However, to the degree that something is sacred, it is to that same degree that Satan wishes for it to be desecrated.

Although the demonic realm is real, we need not live in fear. St. Augustine remarked, "Job was turned over to the devil to be tempted so that, by withstanding the test, he would be a torment to the devil."[13] However, don't dialogue with temptation or imagine that you can dabble in it and step back when you've tasted a reasonable amount. If this is your strategy, you'll always lose. Rather, we ought to remain calm and vigilant, remembering the words of Scripture: "Resist the devil and he will flee from you" (James 4:7).

ACTION

Rarely does sin take control of you in bold, new ways. Sin is welcomed in through smaller entry points that widen over time. What begins with missing Sunday Mass can, over time, turn into an abandonment of one's faith (and values). What starts with a little chemical experimentation often evolves into a full-blown addiction. That one night of blowing off homework, that one day of missed classes, or that occasional drunken hookup might quickly become more of a habit than an exception.

Make a mental list of sins in your life that are often considered "little," such as talking back, negative humor, wasted time on screens, crude language, or degrading music or movies that bring more darkness to you than light. However, don't overwhelm yourself trying to conquer everything today. If your goals are too broad, you'll lose motivation to achieve anything. Rather, focus on battling one of these vices today. As you seal off these entry points and achieve one small victory at a time, the power of lust will gradually diminish. Now, pick one and go after it.

DAY 6

GET TO THE ROOTS

ALL TOO OFTEN, when men attempt to break free from patterns of unwanted sexual behavior or thoughts, they imagine that they should focus on eradicating lust. However, this plan could be compared to the gardener who tries to eliminate weeds by cutting off their leaves. If the root system of a plant remains undisturbed, it will only be a matter of time before it regenerates, resurfaces, and spreads. In the same respect, if a man uses coping mechanisms to keep his desires in check, but never pauses to examine where these desires are coming from, it will only be a matter of time before he relapses and surrenders in resignation, declaring chastity to be an unrealistic, cruel, and unhealthy burden.

In his book *Unwanted*, Jay Stringer offers a profound insight into a man's sexual desires and behaviors: He proposes that our fantasies are often road maps that reveal hurts and unmet needs that have not been addressed in our lives. We spend so much time in a cycle of indulging and repressing our desires that we never sit still long enough to listen to the deeper ache underneath them. He notes, "We are more likely to be ashamed of our unwanted sexual behaviors when we do not understand them."[14] This shame only drives us deeper into isolation, which then makes us all the more susceptible to fall back into our hidden addictions in search of comfort.

For each man, these roots are different. For some, it may be loneliness, rejection, hopelessness, insecurity, a parental wound, neglect, family brokenness, or sexual abuse. Under each of these experiences are legitimate unmet needs that often manifest themselves in the form of various behaviors, fetishes, and addictions. Stringer points out, "Pornography often involves themes of humiliation, violence, and emotional enmeshment because . . . porn users who have endured these traumas will be aroused by the eroticizing of these traumas later in life."[15] For example, if a man desires to control a woman, porn offers him an outlet. Through lust, the man projects his fantasies onto another. She has no mind, personality, or will other than what the man gives her. He has power over her (or so he feels).

However, lust isn't simply a sensual anesthetic used to numb the pain of negative life experiences; sometimes it's a way to recreate the pain and marinate in it. But why would a person do this? Why seek out feelings of defeat, shame, and aloneness? In the movie *The Shawshank Redemption*, one character who had lived for decades in prison committed a crime as soon as freedom was granted to him, because the familiarity of his confinement was more appealing than facing the uncertainty of a life without it. In his mind, a prisoner is *who* he was. So, if a person grows up in a home that is overly rigid, negligent, or abusive, perhaps he identifies with the feelings of shame, emptiness, or self-loathing. Deep down he doesn't see these as feelings he feels, but as proof of who he *is*.

This is why some people repeat patterns of unwanted sexual behavior. Until the deeper wound in their identity is mended, they will continue to immerse themselves in the negative thought patterns associated with it. To deal with our wounds and vices, we might try various methods of sin management, but Jay Stringer points out, "Healing requires you to pivot from condemning your lack of willpower to addressing the role trauma may be playing in your unwanted sexual behavior. A heart with an ounce of kindness for your life story will accomplish so much more for you than a mind filled to the brim with strategies to combat lust."[16] Therefore, instead of seeing our sexual brokenness as an evil problem that needs to be solved, we must open ourselves to the possibility that our wounds can show us the path toward healing.

ACTION

Of all of the readings in this thirty-three-day journey, we invite you to ponder this one more than any other. Take some time to ruminate on this perspective. Do not rush this.

One reason why fantasies are alluring is because they might be taboo, risqué, and illicit. But what would happen if we were allowed—and even encouraged—to think *about* them? To find true sexual healing, we must! In other words, examine the recurring fantasy, desire, or sexual habit instead of merely indulging in it. Ask yourself:

- What is it that I crave?
- Where is this coming from? Why do I desire this? What is driving me? What is behind it?

- When did I begin seeking this out, and what was happening in my life at that time?
- What unmet need within me does it seem to satisfy or temporarily soothe?
- Am I drawn to this through my insecurity because no risk of rejection is involved?
- When I indulge, am I focusing on getting something from the person, or doing something to them? What could this mean?
- Am I sexualizing my anger, eroticizing revenge, or resenting the object of my lust?
- Am I sexualizing my longing for acceptance, admiration, and affection?
- Am I escaping from something?
- What do my desires and behaviors reveal about who I think I am?

Take a moment to pray through this. Slowly bring each of these desires to God, no matter how repulsive or ungodly they might seem to be. This is true prayer. Don't spend this time in mere human introspection. Ask the Holy Spirit to reveal you to yourself. Let God see you and love you, exactly where you're at, so that your true identity as His beloved son can be restored.

This process is not about self-pity, which leads

to a spirit of victimhood and entitlement. It's not about blaming others or our circumstances as an excuse not to mature. It's about being merciful, not pitiful. It's about having the courage to process your wounds instead of becoming the kind of man who passes them on to others.

DAY 7

IDENTIFY YOUR TRIGGERS

A TRIGGER IS something that leads to something else. When it comes to triggers for our temptations, the obvious ones might be an attractive person walking by, an immodest billboard, or an online advertisement inviting us to stare and click. But look deeper. When do you find yourself most tempted? Is it when you're bored, lonely, angry, stressed, or tired? Temptation most often enters when we are physically and emotionally struggling. That is when you're an easy target.

For example, nutritionists often point out that perhaps the most common cause of sugar cravings and hunger pains is dehydration. This happens because when we do not consume enough fluid, it becomes more difficult for the body to metabolize glycogen for energy. Then, we begin to crave a quick source of energy and mistakenly satisfy our true thirst with a sugary snack. But if the deeper need isn't met, the cycle repeats itself.

Likewise, during moments of desolation, we naturally seek consolation. But what we choose for consolation says a great deal about our level of emotional maturity. If we turn to lust to resolve negative feelings, we're using others and stunting our own development as men to manage our struggles.

The next time you feel tempted, pause for a moment and consider your affective state. To do this, use the acronym BLAST (Bored, Lonely, Angry, Stressed, or Tired) to take an inventory of your emotions at the moment. If you recognize one of these triggers, say audibly (though it will feel weird at first) "This is a trigger." By doing this you engage the thinking part of your brain, which will help you to "wake up" and avoid going down that path. Realize the false promise before you. Like an anti-gospel, lust invites men, "Come to me, all you who are weary and heavy laden, and I will give you restlessness."

This helps you regain clarity of thought, so that you're not being led around by your moods and temptations. You're taking the lead. Now, you have the opportunity to listen to that trigger and address the underlying issue. If you notice that you're bored, go do something good, such as exercise. If you're lonely, call a friend or connect with a family member.

If you're angry, find a good outlet for that and talk it through with someone so you can process that emotion in a productive way. If you're stressed, take care of your body and find an activity that relaxes you. If you're tired, take a good look at the amount of sleep you've been giving yourself or just go to bed!

When we're immersed in desolation, temptations appear much more powerful than they really are. When we address the core issues, those temptations might not disappear, but they will become easier to control.

ACTION

When formulating a successful battle plan, one useful strategy is to examine your own reaction sequence that leads to sin. For example:

Time of day	Late at night
Location	Alone in room
Emotion	Bored/stressed
Action that leads to	Surf social media
Setback	Porn

One helpful way to visualize this sequence is to create your own "three-circle plan." This enables you to become aware of the things in your life that strengthen you (outer circle) and the things that require boundaries (middle circle), so that they do not lead to things you should never do (inner circle). You could think of it as a green, yellow, and red light, representing go, caution, and stop.

Below is an example of how this might look.

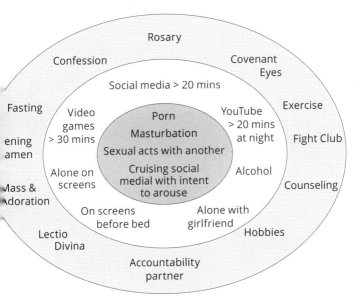

Rosary

Confession

Covenant Eyes

Social media > 20 mins

Fasting

Video games > 30 mins

Porn
Masturbation
Sexual acts with another
Cruising social medial with intent to arouse

YouTube > 20 mins at night

Exercise

ening amen

Fight Club

Alone on screens

Alcohol

Mass & Adoration

Counseling

On screens before bed

Alone with girlfriend

Lectio Divina

Hobbies

Accountability partner

Create your own three-circle plan and then if you have a setback, you can look back to it and see where there was a breakdown and adjust accordingly. The key is to adjust the plan as needed and learn from our mistakes frequently.

DAY 8

RENOUNCE YOUR AFFECTION FOR SIN

FONDNESS. THAT'S THE word that could be used to describe the secret affection we often keep for sins that we claim to be trying to overcome. We fall into sin, experience the emptiness that follows, become frustrated in our inability to conquer the habit, and then attempt to wound the vice. We stab at it, but we don't want to kill it. We've formed a bond, and we want to keep it around in moderation. We hate it but have also come to enjoy it and depend upon it. There's a relationship, an unclean bond that has been created. However, habitual sin makes us increasingly timid in our resolution to sever the bond.

Part of this bond is created because we have fallen into the trap of thinking that it's hell all the way to heaven, and heaven all the way to hell. That is, we wrongly believe that if we're to make it to heaven, it's going to require a life of boredom and repression, whereas hell, on the other hand, will involve a life of pleasure and freedom. This, we must understand, is *absolutely false.* The truth is that "every one who commits sin is a slave to sin" (John 8:34), but "where the Spirit of the Lord is, there is freedom" (2 Cor 3:17). As Jesus said, "The thief comes only to steal and kill and destroy; I came that they may have life, and have it abundantly" (John 10:10). Or in the words of the Psalmist, "Take delight in the Lord, and he will give you the desires of your heart" (Ps 37:4). Until we believe this, we'll never trust God with our bodies.

ACTION

In order to sever a bond with sin, one thing that needs to take place is a firm renunciation of our attachment to it. Granted, more will be required on your part than this, but you may be surprised at the effects of it. To do this, pray with firmness of will the following prayer three times, preferably alone and out loud:

"In the name, power, blood, and authority of Jesus Christ, I bind and rebuke all unclean spirits

that may be afflicting me. I renounce the sins of ____
and I renounce any affection I have retained for
them. I reject the empty promises of Satan, I refuse
to be mastered by sin, and I hereby offer to God
every disordered attachment that keeps me from
Him. Amen."

When you pray this, you may experience a
feeling of joy, deliverance, and freedom, or you
might feel a false sense of sadness, remorse, loss,
or betrayal. You may feel like you're breaking off
an old friendship, severing ties with a companion
who has accompanied you during some dark times.
It's okay to feel that. It's a false attachment, but an
attachment nonetheless. There's no need to grieve
this loss, because the straightest path to God is to
let go of everything that leads you away from Him.

DAY 9

REDEEM FATHERHOOD

IT IS A NATURAL instinct of boys to observe and imitate their fathers. When I (Matt) was growing up, my father discovered that I had a secret stash of porn magazines and he simply gave me a wink and said, "Don't let your mum know." In my case (Jason), I don't recall having a single childhood friend who had not discovered porn on his father's computer or in his nightstand. It was universal. In fact, my best friend's parents in high school paid for him to have a subscription to *Playboy*! I even had one friend whose father took him to a brothel in Mexico as a teenager and congratulated him for becoming a man after they left the establishment.

Exodus 34:7 states that although God is merciful and forgiving, the iniquity of fathers will visit "the children and the children's children, to the third and the fourth generation." In other words, a father's purity—or lack thereof—echoes within his family for generations. However, a father cannot inspire his children to be pure in heart if he is not striving to possess the virtue himself. A boy's natural inclination is to idealize his father, but if a father does not value chastity, the boy will not only excuse himself from making any effort to pursue it, he will instinctively devalue purity and consider it to be an unmanly trait. For him to think otherwise would require him to consider his father to be unmanly, and no impressionable young mind is capable of making such a mature and unbiased conclusion. It would feel disloyal.

But now you have matured. You are capable of realizing that your father may not have been a perfect man. It's time to take an honest look and, if necessary, create a new legacy for future generations.

ACTION

Perhaps you have been blessed with a father who strove for purity of heart, and your only complaint is that he seemed a bit overzealous about his desire for you to do the same. If this is the case, thank God for him. However, if your upbringing more closely resembles the stories above, or your father was simply neglectful in providing you with any guidance about authentic masculinity, we have two challenges for you today:

First: Take some time in prayer right now to consider your memories of your father. Pause after each of the following points and give yourself time to see what surfaces. Think of the ways he interacted with your mother, or with other women. Consider how he looked at women as he drove or walked by them. How did he speak about women? How he did interact with women when your mother was not around? What was his reaction, if anything, to seeing immodest commercials? Did he keep impure magazines out of the house, or welcome them in? Was he secretive about what he was viewing online? Did you ever discover on his computer things that wounded you, or that you were fearful to tell your mother about?

Perhaps these few questions trigger a tsunami of emotional memories, or just a few. Whatever the case may be, we need to contemplate the ways in which we were shaped by our father's actions (or inaction). If those experiences were negative, we must use that angst in a positive manner. We need to begin asking ourselves how our future children would answer those same questions about us, years from now.

Second: We must forgive our fathers. For some, this may be a simple interior act of the will. For others, this might feel impossible. Sometimes a father's abuse or negligence can leave a wound that feels unforgivable. But if we choose to retain the sins of another, we prevent our own healing. We mistakenly believe that if we ever forgive him, then it would somehow minimize the severity of the injury. But this is untrue. Forgiveness is not forgetfulness. Rather, it shows that love is more powerful than sin. If you struggle to let go of past hurts, ask God for the gift of a merciful heart. This may take time, but God will answer that prayer if we have the courage to ask for the grace.

DAY 10

BUILD BROTHERHOOD

ALTHOUGH WE HAD no role in choosing our fathers, we have all the power in the world to decide who our male companions will be. Choosing good men is an essential component of masculine development, because we always become like our friends. If we choose companions who brag about their sexual conquests, trade porn on their phones, and joke about their masturbation habits, we won't stand much of a chance to rise above the bog of impurity we've chosen to immerse ourselves in. We might even think we're advancing in virtue because we're not "as bad" as some of them.

However, when you establish virtuous male friendships, you'll see your faults as clearly as you had previously seen the faults of others. Instead of assuming that you're noble because others are behaving like heathens, you'll realize all the ways in which you need to improve. No one will force you to fellowship with such men; it's your job to find them. Where do you look for them? If you're in high school, talk to your campus minister at school or youth minister at church. If you're in college, connect with the Newman Center or FOCUS team on campus. If you're out of college, reach out to the diocesan director of young adult ministry, and get plugged in to that community. Once you've found that group, immerse yourself in it and become accountable.

When you're connected to a solid band of brothers, they can offer irreplaceable support to help you obtain victory over your vices. Consider, for example, the following exchange that took place between two men. When one confided in the other about his struggle with lust, the accountability partner replied:

> "If what you *really* want to do is look at porn," he said, "then go ahead and look at porn." "Yeah, right. Like I'm really going to do that." I chuckled cynically. Larry just looked at me, dead serious, and repeated himself. "If what you *really* want to do is look at porn and masturbate, then go ahead and do it." I could tell he wasn't being flippant, but I also knew his integrity. So, I launched back at him, "I know this must be come kind of reverse psychology or paradoxi-

cal treatment you're trying on me, right?" The look on his face, however, told me this was not his intention. "I don't get it," I exclaimed. "Why are you telling me to go ahead and look at porn and masturbate?" In frustration, I hit my fist against the armchair and shouted, "That's not what I want to do!" Larry's eyes sparkled with delight. "Exactly!" he cheered. "That's the point. Looking at pornography and masturbating is *not what you really want to do.*" I was speechless. *Could it really be true? Despite my out-of-control passions, could a passion for God inside me run deeper than my desire for sex and porn?*[17]

If we deprive ourselves of authentic brotherhood, we rob ourselves of the opportunity to gain life-changing insights. If you truly desire freedom, don't fight for it alone. As one man remarked, "The opposite of addiction isn't sobriety. It's connection."[18]

ACTION

The best way to make zero progress in battling sins of the flesh is to do it all yourself: Be the hero. Don't answer to anyone and keep your struggles to yourself. Retain your pride and untarnished reputation and let everyone around you think that you've got it all together. Do this, and you'll always show the world a filtered version of yourself, while hiding the real man who surfaces when no one else is watching. There's no need to lead such an exhausting double life. Drop the image campaign and be accountable.

Accountability means being transparent with a trusted friend or mentor about your struggles so that he can offer encouragement and support. It means allowing another person to remind you of who you are and who you desire to be. Therefore, find a friend or mentor you can trust. Ask him to be your accountability partner. Share with this person when you're struggling and how you're progressing. As St. Philip Neri would say, a temptation disclosed is half overcome.[19]

Years ago, it required serious and deliberate effort for a man to obtain pornography. Now, the same level of effort is required *not* to see it! However, if you take advantage of accountability programs like Covenant Eyes (covenanteyes.com), avoiding porn becomes easier. Try it for free for a month using the promo code: chastity. Once downloaded, it will not only block porn, but will send a daily report of your online activity to your accountability partner. (If you're in high school, it's best if this is a parent.) This, in our opinion, is not optional if you're serious about living porn-free. Remember: No recovering porn user can be an island! As the Bible says, "Though a man might prevail against one who is alone, two will withstand him. A threefold cord is not quickly broken" (Eccl 4:12).

DAY 11

BE ABSOLVED

DEEP DOWN, WE know when we're falling short. Think about it: The windows of "adult" bookstores aren't darkened only to protect the innocence of the public; they're also opaque to conceal the identity of the customers. Anonymity makes sin more enticing.

If we're honest with ourselves, we'll admit the truth: God needs to make an extraction in all of us. In the book of Jeremiah, God asks, "How long shall your evil thoughts lodge within you? . . . How long will it be before you are made clean?" (Jer 4:14; 13:27). Although these words from God may seem harsh, have you ever asked yourself the same thing? Have you ever wondered in frustration when you'll finally be free from your struggles? You might feel useless to God and perhaps ruined. However, keep in mind what God says to Jeremiah a few chapters later:

"Arise, and go down to the potter's house, and there I will let you hear my words." So I went down to the potter's house, and there he was working at his wheel. And the vessel he was making of clay was spoiled in the potter's hand, and he reworked it into another vessel, as it seemed good to the potter to do. Then the word of the Lord came to me: "O house of Israel, can I not do with you as this potter has done?" says the Lord. "Behold, like the clay in the potter's hand, so are you in my hand, O house of Israel." (Jer. 18:1–6)

When the clay was spoiled in the hands of the potter, he did not discard it. He reworked it. No matter where you find yourself, you're not beyond the reach of God's mercy if you're willing to accept it. Thankfully, Jesus established a sacrament to bring it to us.

As great as it is to have brothers who know your struggles, the fact remains that they cannot absolve you of your sins. As soon as Jesus rose from the dead, He spoke peace to the apostles and said, "As the Father has sent me, even so I send you." He then breathed on them and said, "Receive the Holy Spirit. If you forgive the sins of any, they are forgiven; if you retain the sins of any, they are retained"

(John 20:21–23). The only other time in Scripture when God breathes on man is at the moment of creation. So, it's clear that something major is happening here. God is breathing the Holy Spirit into the apostles and empowering them to forgive sins, just as He had empowered them to cure the sick, cast out demons, and raise people from the dead.[20]

In confession, we not only receive the gift of forgiveness, we also receive actual graces to avoid those sins in the future. Therefore, if we wish to overcome our vices without *frequently* accessing the graces that await us in the sacrament of reconciliation, we are guilty of self-reliance. Don't deprive yourself: Take advantage of the sacrament at least once per month. To find confession times near you, search your parish website or go to masstimes.org.

ACTION

Not only is it essential to go to confession, it is also important to make a good confession. Here are three steps to do this:

First: Don't priest-hop. In other words, find a solid confessor, and go to him consistently. If you wanted to make progress in any sport, you wouldn't change your coach every few weeks. In the same respect, as a confessor gets to know you and your challenges, he'll be better able to customize the pastoral advice he offers you.

Second: Make a careful examination of your conscience before you enter the confessional. Since you're already doing your evening examen on a daily basis as a part of this program, your examination of conscience will flow naturally from this. If you've fallen out of the habit of doing this nightly, get back on track and retain this as a lifelong devotion.

Third: Be transparent. Think of your soul as a dimly lit room that has been cluttered with debris over time (sin). At times, we glance into the room and grab a few obvious items that need to be discarded and take them to confession. But we know there are corners of that room that we don't want to visit or inspect. They're the darkest places, and perhaps we haven't looked there in years because we'd rather forget what has been concealed there. If there are sins that you have committed that you feel are too shameful to confess, the time has come to allow God's light to shine in that darkness. You do not have to bear the weight of that sin any longer. As soon as you are able, go to confession and say everything. Leave nothing behind. Do this, and you will unleash the full graces that are awaiting you in this wondrous sacrament of mercy.

If you are fearful to do this, reflect deeply upon what St. Claude de la Colombière said about the mercy of God. Read it slowly, and more than one time. Invite the Lord into this moment:

> I glorify you in making known how good you are towards sinners, and that your mercy prevails over all malice, that nothing can destroy it, that no matter how many times or how shamefully we fall, or how criminally, a sinner need not be driven to despair of your pardon. . . . It is in vain that your enemy and mine sets new traps for me every day. He will make me lose everything else before the hope that I have in your mercy.

DAY 12

KEEP TRACK

EVERY SPORTS FRANCHISE has a team of mathematicians who work behind the scenes running analytics to study and improve player performance. Although you could fit all of the data ever collected in the first 135 years of baseball onto a single 2GB flash drive, teams today collect approximately 1TB worth of data from high-speed video and radar every single game![21] Arrive early to an NBA game, and you're likely to see an assistant coach sitting beside a player on the bench, reviewing footage on a tablet that exposes the opponent's strategies. Some NFL athletes have even constructed mobile tech headquarters in their SUVs, so that they can analyze game tape while being driven to practice! There's only one reason why they do this: It works. To succeed in business, you need to inspect what you expect. You need to measure deliverables and diagnose inefficiencies in order to maximize output. If such a model works in sports and finance, it's worth implementing for growth in virtue.

***

ACTION

As we prepare to move with you into the second stage of this program, we want to encourage you to begin tracking your progress. The purpose of this isn't simply to log victories and losses so that you have a record of your successes and setbacks. The goal is to gain a deeper understanding of influential factors that may be underlying your struggles. For example, tracking might reveal that you often fall into lustful habits when you're home alone after work or school, or when you're feeling angry or bored. If you know where your fortress's defenses are weakest, you'll know where the walls need to be reinforced.

To track your progress, it's ideal to have a tool that's just as persistent and mobile as the lustful offerings on a cell phone. Thankfully, there's an app for that, and it's password protected. With it, you can receive free and robust tracking of your daily fight against sin. You can set check-in reminders throughout the day, view and add setbacks or confessions in the calendar, discover triggers and go straight to suggested content for each trigger, and even journal directly in the app, keeping a record of your march toward victory.

In the struggle for purity, accountability is one of the greatest weapons we can have in our arsenal—that's why accountability is a key feature on the app. There's a way for you to invite close friends into your walk. Through it, you'll be able to quickly send out a subtle prayer request when you need it the most. You can send up a flare for support and know confidently that you are not alone. Take advantage of this and download it today through the link at chastity.com/forged.

DAY 13

GUARD YOUR PEACE

"THE FIRST GOAL of spiritual combat," according to Fr. Jacques Philippe, "is not to always obtain a victory (over our temptations, our weaknesses, etc.), rather it is to learn to maintain peace of heart under all circumstances, even in the case of defeat."[22] The battle for purity of heart is a long one, and if any man enters into this arena expecting to be unscathed, he'll inevitably surrender to discouragement. In fact, the man who makes moral flawlessness his goal will fall into despair as quickly as an athlete who expects never to face defeat.

Granted, it's reasonable to feel frustrated when you've been trying for months or years to overcome a vice, and it always seems to prevail. But even if the battle is long, there's no reason to lose your peace. St. Padre Pio pointed out:

The spirit of God is a spirit of peace. Even in the most serious faults He makes us feel a sorrow that is tranquil, humble, and confident and this is precisely because of His mercy. The spirit of the devil, instead, excites, exasperates, and make us feel, in that very sorrow [for our sins], anger against ourselves, whereas we should, on the contrary, be charitable with ourselves first and foremost. Therefore, if any thought agitates you, this agitation never comes from God, who gives you peace, being the Spirit of Peace, but from the devil.[23]

Recognize discouragement as a temptation in itself, and reject it. Even if you've been to confession numerous times for the same sin, don't forget that holiness is achieved through the struggle, not by the absence of it.

If and when we fall, we need to avoid two extremes: The first is indifference and the second is discouragement. When we are tempted to commit a serious sin, like fornication, pornography, or masturbation, God says, "Remember my judgment," while the devil says, "Remember God's mercy." After the sin has been committed, however, the opposite is true; God says, "Remember my mercy," while Satan says, "Remember God's judgement!" In other words, prior to the sin,

Satan minimizes it and reassures us that it's not worth being so scrupulous about. After the sin, his comfort turns to condemnation! At such moments, remember he is the father of lies. Make a firm act of the will to trust in God's mercy rather than in your own perfection. And in the meantime, keep in mind that lust isn't the only sin you should focus on in your life.

If you're struggling in a particular area of lust, such as masturbation, set reachable goals for overcoming the habit. For example: "I'm going to go one week without doing it," and go from there. As you win one small battle at a time, you'll discover that you will not only grow in respect for women, you'll also feel more respect for yourself as you grow in confidence and self-mastery.

ACTION

When you fail in your resolutions to live a pure life, do you struggle with discouragement? If we are surprised by our frailty, it's often a sign of pride. What reason do we have to be so astonished that we're imperfect?

Other times, our discouragement reveals a deeper wound. It may be that we've inherited a flawed image of God as a distant Father who is difficult to please and is forever dissatisfied with our imperfect efforts. We mistakenly think that His love is conditional and that His affection needs to be earned. It's a performance-based relationship.

It doesn't take much effort to see where this image of God may have developed. It has been said that our relationship with God begins where our relationship with our earthly father leaves off. Take a moment to consider if you have projected onto God some of the shortcomings of your dad. If this exercise brings to mind certain hurts, pause. Allow those memories and emotions to surface.

As men, we're encouraged to be unemotional. But it isn't manly to act numb and emotionlessness. It's fearful. Allow yourself to feel sadness, anger, disappointment, or whatever corresponds with your experience. Try to recall specific instances when you felt that you needed to earn your father's love, or instances when he seemed unavailable. Invite God into each of those memories, to bring healing. Then, take time in prayer to give God a chance to gradually reveal His affection for you. Eventually, you will be able to distinguish His perfect love for you from the imperfect love that you experienced elsewhere.

PART TWO

THE HAMMER AND ANVIL:
SHAPED FOR A PURPOSE

THE PREVIOUS TEN days have likely been intense for you. We've taken a deep dive into what's driving you. You might not necessarily feel stronger, and that's to be expected. The intention was to make your heart malleable, so that it could more easily be formed.

As we mentioned earlier, the first stage of the forging process is the furnace. When the metal is removed from the heat, it is temporarily softer. The glowing orange steel is then placed upon an anvil and the blacksmith's hammer shapes it for its purpose. In the same manner, the following ten days will be a time of formation. The ultimate goal of purity is to free you to love, and so the following strategies for combating lust will guide you toward this purpose and will be useful throughout your lifetime.

As you begin this second phase of the book, remain in contact with your accountability partner and persevere in your *Lectio Divina* and evening examen. However, instead of praying one Hail Mary per day, offer a daily decade (ten Hail Marys) to her.

DAY 14

STRUGGLE WITH LUST

MANY OF US use the word "struggle" as if it were synonymous with "give in to." We hear people say, "I've been struggling with masturbation," and we assume they mean "I've been giving in to masturbation," and that *is* what they mean; but that's not what "struggle" means. To struggle means "to contend with an adversary or opposing force." This is true in all aspects of life. In war, the goal of a soldier is not to get rid of battles, but to win them. He could get rid of them by surrendering every time. In weight lifting, resistance builds strength. Without an opposing force, growth doesn't happen.

One reason why temptation is so alluring is because the rewards of chastity are not immediate. One might think, "Okay, I didn't lust after her . . . now what? If I give in, at least I'll get something right now." While purity may feel like a pointless act of self-denial in the moment, authentic masculinity emerges from these hidden sacrifices, which are especially pleasing to God.

No matter what, success requires struggle. Therefore, if you are tempted to lust, we hope you won't take offense when we say that we hope you struggle with it! As desperate as our situation may sometimes seem, we need to recognize that this is not just a struggle; it is an opportunity to access a massive outpouring of God's grace. Think about it: the men who fought for their purity in every era before the internet existed never had the opportunity to contend with and defeat the foe you face daily. Sure, they had their own share of temptations, but the availability and anonymity of lust offered online today is unprecedented.

But there's no need to be discouraged about this and surrender to self-pity. St. Paul assures us that "where sin increased, grace abounded all the more" (Rom 5:20). This means that unique graces are being offered in our time. Are you taking advantage of them?

ACTION

In November 1830, the Blessed Virgin Mary appeared to St. Catherine Labouré during her evening prayer time in the chapel. She recalled, "Her face was totally beautiful, I could not describe it. And then, all of a sudden, I noticed rings on her fingers, rings with precious stones, some larger and some smaller, which gave out rays of light some more beautiful than others . . . the glitter from the rays of light were so magnificent." Our Lady said to her, "This is the symbol of the graces which I will pour out upon the persons who ask them of me." St. Catherine noticed that some of the jewels did not cast any rays. The Virgin Mary explained, "Those stones which remained in the shadows represent the graces which people forgot to ask of me."[24]

How often do we struggle with various vices, addictions, or difficult situations without seeking divine assistance? If we are going to overcome our struggles, we need to tap into the ocean of graces that God offers us at every moment. Right now, ask Our Lord and Our Lady for those graces you forget to ask for. If you're struggling with impurity, ask for purity. If you struggle with despair, ask for hope.

If you struggle with selfishness, ask for a selfless heart. If you're struggling with addiction, pray for deliverance. Granted, virtues take time to develop. But God promises, "Ask, and it will be given you; seek, and you will find; knock, and it will be opened to you. For every one who asks receives, and he who seeks finds, and to him who knocks it will be opened" (Luke 11:9–10).

DAY 15

FLEE IDLENESS

IN PSALM 51, King David cries out to God to have mercy on him, to blot out his transgressions, wash him from his iniquity, cleanse him from sin, purge him, wash him, and deliver him from "bloodguiltiness." He begs God for mercy, for a clean heart, and for a new spirit to be placed within him, adding: "For I know my transgressions, and my sin is ever before me. Against thee, thee only, have I sinned, and done that which is evil in thy sight" (Ps 51: 3–4). What could David have done to have filled him with such remorse?

As you may know, he committed adultery, impregnated his mistress, and murdered her husband. But what set all of these terrible choices into motion? Idleness. The story begins in 2 Samuel 11, which reads:

In the spring of the year, the time when kings go forth to battle, David sent Jo'ab, and his servants with him, and all Israel; and they ravaged the Ammonites, and besieged Rabbah. But David remained at Jerusalem. It happened, late one afternoon, when David arose from his couch and was walking upon the roof of the king's house, that he saw from the roof a woman bathing; and the woman was very beautiful. And David sent and inquired about the woman.

Follow the cascade of events closely: Spring was the time of year when kings went to war, but King David stayed home, taking a late-afternoon nap and strolling on his rooftop while lusting after another man's wife. His servants informed him she was already married to Uriah, but he sent for her nonetheless.

Mortal sin is never an isolated event. It's always the end result of a litany of missed opportunities to make better decisions. And more times than not, the one domino that begins the chain reaction is idleness. King David could have gone to battle with his troops and should have been off the couch, doing something for his kingdom. He could have looked away when he saw the woman and left it there. But he requested to learn about her and knowingly committed adultery, and then arranged the murder of one of his loyal soldiers! For good reason, St. John Bosco said, "The principal trap that the devil sets for young people is idleness. This is a fatal source of all evil. Don't let there be any doubt in your mind that man is born to work, and when he doesn't do so, he's out of his element and in great danger of offending God."[25]

ACTION

One of the allurements of lust is that it requires little effort or risk. When a man views porn, the woman online will never reject him. When a man goes "too far" with his girlfriend, he exerts no effort to curb his desire. When someone turns to masturbation, all that's required of him is to yield to his urges. Whereas purity requires effort and toil, passivity is common to all acts of lust.

Therefore, a man must use the power of his will, and especially the deep convictions of his heart to counteract this passivity. The best time to do this is not in the midst of a powerful temptation, but long before it has the chance to take root. How do you do this? Stay busy! After all, only a boring person experiences boredom. Instead of sitting around and waiting to be entertained, choose to create, serve, learn, pray, build, or exercise. Just do something!

Granted, it's not healthy to work incessantly. Time for recreation is essential. But when the time comes for that, make sure it's an activity that truly re-creates you, rather than something that wastes time and leaves you feeling restless. In fact, take some time today to do something good that you truly enjoy! You're about halfway through the program, so reward yourself for the effort. Purity involves living a balanced life, not one of mere drudgery and deprivation.

DAY 16

STARVE YOUR LUST

A TEENAGE GIRL once told me (Matt) that her battle with porn felt like battling a sumo wrestler. "I don't stand a chance," she said. "What if you could starve the sumo?" I asked. "Granted, it's a weird thought experiment, but humor me." "Well," she thought, "I guess eventually he would lose his strength and I, provided I was taking care of myself, would gain strength and, eventually, overcome." Precisely.

The same is true with lust. How do we starve the sumo—the temptation to look at porn, go too far with a girlfriend, or allow our imagination to wander where it shouldn't? Primarily through the senses. St. John Chrysostom compared our five senses (taste, touch, smell, hearing, and sight) to the entry points of a majestic castle. You must guard those entry points and protect your castle from the enemy at all costs. The devil will use every means and take any opportunity to derail our pursuit of sanctity; he uses anything he can within creation to turn us away from the Creator. Those things we can taste, touch, see, hear, and smell can either pull us toward darkness or inspire us to run toward the light.

If we think that small indiscretions are insignificant, remember how sin works. Smaller sins become friends over time and, unless they are dealt with quickly and directly, they develop into friends that you not only entertain but that you practically invite to move into the bedroom of your mind and heart. Once there, they grow, set up shop in your life, and lay roots in your soul. The snowball of shame and guilt will grow heavier until your moral compass is pointing only toward self. All of a sudden, as you seek to protect sinful desires and justify destructive habits, the beauty and peace you knew on your last retreat, camp, or conference weekend are labeled as "just a phase." To prevent this, secure your fortress.

ACTION

The devil tends to enter through the doors we purposely leave open. Consider where your entry points are for the evil one. What "doors to your soul" do you intentionally leave open to sin? Do you stay up late with no one else around? Do you have certain sites or favorite apps that only put more temptation in your path? Are your favorite shows or movies leading you toward light or surrounding you with darkness?

Therefore, focus on guarding your senses today, especially through sight and sound. Don't take part in impure conversations. Either change the subject or leave. Skip songs, shows, movies, and apps that degrade the gift of sexuality. Eventually, the temptation to look at porn will weaken, you will grow stronger, and you will find yourself overcoming more often than losing the fight.

To begin securing the doors of your soul, take a moment on your phone, your computer, and in your room to delete and eliminate any entry points. Shut the door of your heart (and your bedroom) to the devil and bar it closed. There's no need to make your battle more difficult. When it comes to porn or swimsuit magazines, you can't keep your favorites. Without a final peek, everything has to go. This may feel painful, but that's because we've allowed our senses to become gluttons for lust. We've trained them to look at and listen to everything that might possibly arouse them. As St.

Gregory the Great said, "When a taste for sinful pleasures takes possession of a heart, it thinks of nothing but how to gratify its inordinate desires."[26]

If you need a specific place to start, here's an idea: Depending upon what your audio library looks like, this one might hurt, but we promise that you will not die: Delete from your phone every song that degrades women. If you're unsure if it's degrading, imagine singing the lyrics to your mom and see if that clears things up.

DAY 17

MANAGE WITHDRAWAL

SOME PEOPLE WHO are trying to break free from lust overspiritualize the matter. In other words, they look for solutions that are entirely religious in nature and focus only on caring for the soul. They overlook physiology and psychology and make limited progress as a result. For this reason, we need to take a fully human approach to healing our addictions; one that cares for the body as well as the soul.

While some might object "I'm not really addicted," others might argue that they can't stop "because I'm addicted." In either case, addiction should not be defined as how frequently a person indulges in a compulsion (for example, once a day or once a week). Rather, addiction is better measured by a person's inability to resist the desire to indulge, whenever the compulsion arises (whether it be once a day or once a year).

When people seek to overcome any addiction, they often note that the first few weeks of recovery are the most difficult. Gradually, the urge to relapse lessens. But like a pair of magnets, the pull is strongest when the two objects are closest.

The findings of modern neuroscience are now explaining in scientific language what those of us who have been addicted to anything already know: The addictive state leaves us in constant craving for a neurochemical "cocktail" (endorphins, dopamine, serotonin, etc.) that, with compulsive use, effectively resets the pleasure thermostat of our brain. The result is that alcoholics need more booze, drug addicts need bigger hits, and porn users need more and harder kinds of sexual stimulation—just to feel "normal." In the words of C. S. Lewis, the devil's formula is to create within us "an ever increasing craving for an ever diminishing pleasure."[27]

When one pulls away from this habitual neurochemical reward system, the neural pathways need to be reset. At first, the absence of the stimuli might seem distracting, unbearable, or even cruel. The temptation might be to think: "It's not realistic to stop 'cold turkey,' so perhaps I should just gradually wean myself from lust." This is a trap, because the longer you take to remove an addiction, the deeper its hooks will sink into you. What's needed is to replicate the neurochemical reward in a healthy way. Here's how:

ACTION

St. Paul, who understood well the lures and temptations of the world, reminded us that God will always provide for us a way out if we call upon Him: "No temptation has overtaken you that is not common to man. God is faithful, and He will not let you be tempted beyond your strength, but with the temptation will also provide the way of escape, that you may be able to endure it" (1 Cor 10:13). No matter how strong they may seem, your temptations are not uniquely irresistible. They are common to man—and so are the graces that God offers you to overcome them.

God isn't saying that situations aren't tempting. He knows better than we do the methods and strategies of the devil. God was there in Eden during the Fall and first sin. Likewise, the devil tempted Jesus face-to-face in the desert.[28] What God is saying through St. Paul is that *if we have the presence of mind and humility of heart to call upon Him*, we can withstand any temptation that comes our way. He has not created man in such a way that we will spontaneously combust if we don't relieve our lust.

One of the best ways to redirect your energy in a positive way is through vigorous exercise. By this, we don't mean ten push-ups. Rather, by truly exerting yourself through a single challenging workout or run, your brain will produce significant mood-altering neurochemicals such as dopamine, norepinephrine, serotonin, and endogenous opioids.[29] Some days are going to be more challenging than others in this battle. Realize it and accept it. If you're feeling weak today, make some time to exercise. Whatever you do, do *something* physical to exert energy in a positive way.

However, self-care doesn't only mean exercise. Get the sleep you need. Learn how to relax and get outdoors to experience the beauty of creation. Whatever you do, remember that your body and soul are connected. When you're feeling weak, do something about it that won't leave you feeling heavy or ashamed.

DAY 18

FUEL YOUR DESIRE

THINK ABOUT IT: Crash diets don't work. If a man loves buffalo wings and donuts, he has the choice: control his flesh or schedule the angioplasty. Simply eliminating the temptation isn't enough; the body must be retrained, and self-control must come into play. The deeper desires need to be tapped into, as a wellspring of motivation and purpose.

The same is true in the battle for purity. In order to overcome any desire, we need a stronger one. Therefore, if we plan to "starve the sumo" by practicing custody of our senses, the necessary countermeasure to this strategy is to fuel our desire for authentic love. To the extent that we fill our hearts and minds with good things, there will be less room for evil.

Nonetheless, a battle will remain. Even St. Paul lamented the struggle within himself:

I do not understand my own actions. For I do not do what I want, but I do the very thing I hate. . . . I can will what is right, but I cannot do it. For I do not do the good I want, but the evil I do not want is what I do. . . . For I delight in the law of God, in my inmost self, but I see in my members another law at war with the law of my mind and making me captive to the law of sin which dwells in my members. (Rom. 7:15–23)

If you sense such a conflict within you, don't be disturbed. St. Leo the Great said, "Virtue is nothing without the trial of temptation, for there is no conflict without an enemy, no victory without strife."[30] Like everyone, you are a sexual being who wrestles with the effects of original sin. Your body was created with sexual desires for a reason, a purpose. However, the fact that you were created with such desires doesn't mean those desires should dictate your life.

What's needed to guide those desires is the virtue of chastity. This means the proper integration of body and soul, flesh and spirit. Its purpose is not to annihilate your passions but to direct them toward what is true, good, and beautiful. If you allow your soul to lead your body, you'll notice how much more clearly you view temptation and sinful environments. However, in order for our soul to effectively do this, it needs to be formed well. It needs to be fueled. Here's how to do this:

ACTION

If you recall our action item from two days ago, we challenged you to delete degrading content from your phone. Do the same in reverse now. Consider ways in which you can flood your senses with sights and sounds that will lift your heart and mind to God. For example, look up sacred images on your computer or phone and use one of them for the homepage or lock screen. Watch uplifting movies. If you're not sure if a show is worth watching, review it first on a site such as pluggedin.com. Also, find music that lifts you up rather than pulls you down. That doesn't mean it has to be gospel music, but if you've written off Christian musicians in the past, you may be surprised by the extraordinary talent you can find among them in a wide variety of genres.

Although more garbage than ever is available through technology, there is also an unprecedented amount of inspirational content, homilies, apps, and podcasts at your disposal. Therefore, transform your devices into occasions of grace and growth. What had previously been a portal for evil can become a pathway to grace! (To start, check out the prayer apps at chastity.com/forged.)

Also, to fuel your desire for virtue, consider again why you want to make such sacrifices. It's not meaningless self-denial. This is training you to love your future bride and to become the kind of man whose children will want to emulate him. Or, perhaps your self-mastery is a way for you to give yourself fully to the Church through service or a religious vocation. No matter what your motivation, recall the words of St. Ephraem, who said: "In your strife with the devil, you have for spectators the angels and the Lord of angels."[31]

DAY 19

PRAY FOR YOUR TEMPTATIONS

WE HAD MENTIONED an unusual thing earlier in this book—that we hope this program would *increase* your love for porn stars. That might sound strange if we don't define what is meant by "love." Love, St. Thomas Aquinas teaches, is to will the good of the other; to want what is best for him or her. And porn is not what is best for porn stars.

Just as death is the separation of body and soul, the death of love occurs when we separate a woman's body from the woman herself. It's a reduction of the person to her sexual value. In order to love rightly, we need to see more of her. We need to see that she's someone's daughter, someone's sister, someone's mother. Odds are, she has a tragic story. One *Playboy* model said, "It took me close to twenty years, to undo what was done to me in pornography." She knew of another woman in the industry who had to have "her reproductive organs removed because of venereal disease."

After tracking the deaths of 129 porn stars over a period of roughly twenty years, one man discovered that while the average life expectancy of an average person was seventy-eight years, the average life expectancy of these "adult performers" was thirty-seven years.[32] Following the death of these individuals, their images and videos were not removed online. It's not unreasonable—though it is disturbing—to think that many people today will lust over images and videos of men and women whose bodies are decomposing underground.

Though the porn industry would have us believe that the life of a porn performer is glamorous, the statistics and anecdotal evidence simply do not bear this out. As one psychotherapist who specializes in sexual trauma put it:

The experience I find most common among the performers is that they have to be drunk, high, or dissociated in order to go to work. Their . . . terrible work life is often followed by an equally terrible home life. They have an increased risk of sexually transmitted disease (including HIV), domestic violence and have about a 25% chance of making a marriage that lasts as long as three years.[33]

The reason why we encourage you to love porn stars is because beauty is an invitation to love. Loving the people in the porn industry and feeling a profound sense of responsibility (and pity) for them is the only way to overcome the urge to use them. In fact, Pope St. John Paul II once wrote, "The greater the feeling of responsibility for the person the more true love there is."[34] You were made for more than porn, and so were they. Instead of fueling an industry that harms men and women, use your strength for good. For starters, show your love for porn stars by not looking at porn. Sure, they may never know you made this sacrifice, but the Lord will.

ACTION

When you see a seductive image, your initial urge is to be united to the person. You're drawn in and allured. You desire closeness and intimacy, to see and be seen. But when you're striving toward purity you tend to think: "Wait. Can't go there! Nope. I need to think of something else." But what if God does want you to experience union and love with that individual? What if God's ultimate plan for you and that person is that you both stand before Him in all the beauty of your glorified bodies, untied and ablaze in divine love for each other and God, rapt in ecstatic praise before the blissful revelation of the Most Blessed Trinity surrounded by a host of holy angels for all eternity?

That is His plan! You have been created for union with beauty. But if we're only taught to repress and deny our urges, we'll never integrate them in a healthy way. We must learn how to listen to those urges and respond to them in love, instead of burying or blindly obeying them. So, how does a man do this when he sees a pornographic ad or when he has an unexpected mental flashback of a woman he used (or was used by) ten years ago?

Transform temptation with intercession. Refuse to use the individual, and immediately pray for that person: Pray a decade of the rosary, fast, or offer your next Mass for him or her. Respond in love! God will answer you with an outpouring of grace into that person's life that would not have been unleashed had you not interceded for him or her. Every one of these prayers and sacrifices will be unveiled to them in the life to come, when everything that is hidden will come to the light.

DAY 20

SACRIFICE YOUR DESIRE TO BE TEMPTED

WHEN JESUS ENTERED the Garden of Gethsemane with his closest disciples on the night before he died, he encouraged them to "pray that you may not enter into temptation." He then withdrew from them a short distance to pray and returned to again exhort them: "Pray that you may not enter into temptation" (Luke 22: 40, 46). This is an interesting request, considering that five chapters earlier, he told them, "Temptations to sin are sure to come" (Luke 17:1). Why would he tell his followers to pray to avoid something that it sure to come?

Temptation is inevitable, but the amount of temptation we experience can be mitigated by our choices as well as by our prayers. Although it is good to pray during temptation for the strength to resist it, it is far more effective to pray to avoid the temptation altogether. However, let's be honest with ourselves: We don't want to avoid it. We would prefer to experience temptation, savor it for a moment, and then exercise heroic willpower to overcome it.

This is the pride that comes before the fall. When pursuing purity, a man's greatest strength is realizing his weakness. It has been said that as the chain of a rosary joins all the beads, humility sustains all the virtues. Similarly, pride sustains all vices.

ACTION

If you know you're likely to experience temptation in a particular location, one solution is to avoid the place. But sometimes this isn't always possible. Therefore, consider offering a prayer before you go. For example, I (Jason) once worked out at a gym where there was a particular woman who was distractingly attractive and immodest. I made an effort to practice custody of my eyes and would pray for her on occasion.

However, as I was entering the facility one day, I felt prompted to begin praying the Our Father, which includes the petition that we not be led into temptation. I took up the habit of doing this before my workouts, and a curious thing happened: The woman disappeared. She must have moved or quit the gym, because I never saw her again. Now, we can't expect this to always happen, but I think it was God's way of saying that He's happy to grant us special graces when we acknowledge our weakness.

In the end, the goal of purity isn't to avoid seeing attractive women. The goal is to learn how to see them and love them as God does. But in this journey toward purity of heart, we would do well to ask Him for the special grace to avoid temptation.

To apply this in your life, think of the times and places you're likely to be tempted. Is it at school, in a particular class? Is it while you're at work, when a certain colleague is around? Perhaps it's when you're online doing work and are tempted to look at other things. If you sincerely wish to grow in purity, then it's time to offer up as a sacrifice to God your desire to be tempted.

DAY 21

AVOID THE LOCATION OF SIN

A FRIEND OF ours, who had been a youth minister in California, remembers hearing a knock at his door one Sunday afternoon. A discouraged teen plopped down on the youth group couch before him and the following conversation unfolded:

"Chris, I feel really bad."

"What happened?"

"I went over to my girlfriend's house when her parents weren't there, and we ended up having sex."

"OK, go to confession, and then don't go to her parents' house when they're not there."

"That's a good idea."

A week later, the same teen returned, having

fallen into the same sin at the same place. Chris reiterated the advice previously offered, to which the teen replied, "Oh yeah. That's a really good point." A week passed, and the story repeated itself. At this point, Chris gently asked him, "When are you going to get it? You're not strong enough to be alone with her."

Spiritual writers often preach on the need to avoid the near *occasion* of sin. In other words, if we wish to progress in the Christian life, we ought to avoid situations that will inevitably expose us to temptation. But let's get more specific. What is your *location* of sin? Is it at your girlfriend's dorm after ten o'clock at night or when her roommate is away for the weekend? Is it in your bedroom when you have free time after class or work? Is it in the shower, first thing in the morning, or when using the restroom with your cell phone? Or is it in bed, when you're having a difficult time falling asleep? There's no use in formulating a successful battle plan if we don't first locate the battlefield. What's the point of showing up to combat an opponent if their troops are hundreds of miles away?

ACTION

It's easier to prevent a burglary by locking a door than it is to stop an armed robbery in progress. In the same respect, temptation is easier to overcome when you're still at a distance. Therefore, identify your location(s) of sin and redeem them:

If it's at your girlfriend's dorm or home, spend more time in public with her, and avoid late nights alone. If she's going to be your wife one day, then you can look forward to sharing plenty of alone time with her within the sacrament of marriage. But if she's not your wife, don't treat her like one.

If you fall when you're in your room when you have free time after class or work, fill that time with something else. Plan your workouts then. Go for a jog. Spend time with friends and avoid boredom.

If you tend to be most tempted in the shower make the sign of the cross before you get in, and when you feel tempted, raise your heart and mind to God and ask for the grace to remain pure. Take a cold shower every now and then and offer up that discomfort as a prayer for something specific, such as the women trapped in the sex-trade industry, or the conversion of child abusers. This not only brings good out of a moment of temptation, it also reminds your body that you are the master of its desires, not vice versa.

If your location of temptation is the bathroom when you're alone with your phone, quit bringing the phone with you there or leave it in your pocket. You won't die if you spend four minutes without a screen.

If your weakness is bedtime, get into a new routine. To do this, take advantage of the Church's sacramentals! Bless yourself with holy water and do your night prayers immediately before going to rest. Create a visible place for prayer in your room and use it daily. Make the sign of the cross when you're tempted. Wear a Benedictine medal, Miraculous Medal, or crucifix. Hold a rosary. Place some holy images on your nightstand. These are not superstitious trinkets. Exorcists use them for a reason. If you struggle to fall asleep, examine what might be causing your restlessness and try to address that separately, rather than turning to lust to calm your mind.

DAY 22

QUIT
JUSTIFYING

YOU'LL NEVER FIND yourself making an excuse for doing what's right. However, when we do something we shouldn't, we fabricate an endless litany of justifications in an effort to appease our troubled consciences. Here's a list of some of the games we play with ourselves:

I'm not actually looking for porn on that social media app. Sure, I know some bad images pop up sometimes [always] when I'm scrolling around. But it's not like I'm searching them out. It's not my fault if they show up. I'm looking for other stuff.

Yeah, I look at some sites, but it's only for a few minutes once in a while. It's not like I'm forcing women into that industry. If they're willing to do that online, then that's their choice. Why can't I just appreciate the beauty of womanhood? What I do in the privacy of my room isn't hurting anyone.

Sure, I masturbate from time to time, but it's not like I'm addicted. I could stop if I really wanted to. Besides, every guy does it. What does God expect? I need an outlet and it provides harmless relief. It's not like I'm actually doing it and using a woman. Relax: there are plenty of other people in the world doing worse things.

I know things have gotten pretty physical with my girlfriend, but it's not like that's all there is to our relationship. It's not like we just met, or we're having some meaningless hookup. Besides, we're not twelve years old anymore. I can really see myself marrying her one day. If she's okay with it, what's the problem?

Sound familiar? If you recognize these justifications as things you've said to yourself, you're not alone. Virtually every man has wrestled with them. But one of the traits of authentic masculinity and leadership is radical ownership of one's actions. This means that a true man does not shift blame, justify faults, make excuses, or minimize his own shortcomings. Rather, he accepts responsibility for what goes wrong instead of only grasping for the credit when things go right. If we're going to grow into mature Christian men, it's time to identify and remove the justifications we use to guard our sins.

It's also worthwhile to remember that justifications are often based on false assumptions. For example, men who view porn assume that every woman is willing to be filmed. However, one famous porn model said, "Virtually every time someone watches that film, they are watching me being raped."[35] Furthermore, the porn industry is largely fueled by means of human trafficking. It's convenient for porn users to assume these victims are willing, so that they can spare themselves the effort of doing something heroic to end such injustice.

ACTION

The list of justifications above are a good place to start, but now is the time to identify your own. To do this, look at three separate categories of sin: impurity with yourself, impurity online, and impurity with another person. Some men may struggle with all three equally, but often one or two areas are predominant. What is it for you? Take some time to consider what it may be and examine every imaginable reason why you have excused this behavior. Right now, take out a piece of paper and see how many reasons you can accumulate.

In writing them down, you will likely see that some of these rationalizations are particularly weak. You intuit immediately that it's a lame excuse. Some of the others, however, might feel justifiable. That's okay. Just write them down.

Once you've done this, read through them all. Start drawing a line through the excuses that you can most easily reject because of how weak they are. Now, look at what remains. These are the ones you want to bring to prayer and wrestle with God about. Tell Him these reasons. Real prayer is raw, honest, and sometimes messy. Go there with Him. For example, if you feel that God is being unfair by expecting you to let go of a particular sin, tell Him that! If you feel like you deserve some indulgence because of how good you've been otherwise, say that! (In doing this, you may come to discover that many of our excuses are often wrapped up in self-pity.)

After you've expressed yourself to God in prayer, take time to listen as well. Allow Him to work through that with you. In order for Christian prayer to develop from a monologue into a dialogue, you must make time to listen. What God says to you through this exercise will be far more important that anything we could offer.

DAY 23

CONSIDER COUNSELING

SITTING IN THE passenger seat of my mom's minivan, I (Jason) recall as a child witnessing the car in front of us slamming into a vehicle that had already stopped at a red light. The driver who caused the accident stumbled out of his car, bleeding profusely from facial trauma. He opened his back door, removed a cooler, and proceeded to walk through traffic, dumping the evidence of his intoxication into a ditch. He then walked away from the scene of the accident as if he had nothing to do with it and was feeling quite well. My mother, who was a nurse, pursued him and after much negotiation was able to coax him to sit down and wait for the paramedics to arrive. It was astonishing to walk beside her, listening to him explain why he didn't need any help.

Could he have survived without going to the hospital? Probably. One can live with facial lacerations, cracked ribs, and a concussion. But life would be unnecessarily difficult and scar tissue would be evident. In the same manner, when men suffer serious wounds that relate to their sexuality, such as addiction and sexual abuse, but do not pursue counseling, they only make their own lives and relationships more difficult.

Consider the challenges that come when a male has been sexually abused. All too often, men are overlooked when such abuse is discussed. Those who have suffered through it often conceal the injury due to shame. For example, at the age of seven, Mike Tyson was molested by an older man but did not share publicly about the abuse until he was nearly fifty years old. When asked about the impact this experience had on him, he said, "It made me have to be tough for the world I lived in."[36]

While abuse can drive some men toward violence, others withdraw. Researchers from the University of Texas Southwestern Medical School discovered that abuse leads to high levels of stress that trigger excessive levels of brain-derived neurotrophic factor (BDNF) to be released in the brain. When this happens, certain genes in the brain are turned on, causing the victim of abuse to experience social withdrawal, depression, fearfulness, an increased tendency toward addictive behaviors, and a decreased ability to enjoy intimacy in the future.[37] This domino effect of negative consequences doesn't need to ruin a man's future. Whether the wound is abuse or addiction, counseling can mitigate and reverse its effects.

Strictly speaking, it isn't necessary to find a therapist to hash out painful memories and frustrating patterns of self-defeating behavior. But consider how kings, presidents, and prime ministers always surround themselves with advisers who guide them on issues related to foreign diplomacy, economics, military intelligence, and so on. They welcome such counsel because it will exponentially improve their effectiveness as leaders. In the same respect, when a man puts aside his ego and fear, and overcomes the stereotypical stigma associated with seeking help as a man, he will reap the rewards of his humility and courage.

ACTION

If you have suffered sexual abuse, developed an unhealthy pattern of sexual behavior, or are experiencing excessive shame or compulsive and unwanted desires, don't allow fear to prevent you from receiving the healing you deserve.

Some men enter marriage or the priesthood, assuming that their vocation will have the power to magically erase their woundedness. But more often than not, these vocations only magnify one's brokenness. For this reason, one of the greatest gifts you could give yourself (and your future spouse) is the gift of wholeness and healing.

People often find relief in sharing certain wounds with a friend or family member. While this is a good start, think of it like sharing the news of a broken foot with a friend. He could offer some empathy and drive you to the hospital, but you're better off not expecting him to operate on you. To find a good therapist, go to chastity.com/forged to see a list of our recommendations.

PART THREE

THE GRINDING STONE:
POLISHED FOR PERFECTION

ONCE A SWORD has endured the heat of the furnace and the pounding of a hammer upon the anvil, the blacksmith grinds, sharpens, and polishes its blade to make it ready for battle. In the previous weeks, we have offered many physical, psychological, and spiritual strategies that are largely defensive (and reparative) against lust. But the Christian life should not be lived primarily in in a defensive posture. Granted, Scripture speaks of faith as a shield. But it also describes God's word as a sword. In this final phase of our journey together, you will be armed with an arsenal of new weapons for the battles to come.

As you begin this final stage of the program, don't lose touch with your brothers or allow your daily devotions to *Lectio Divina* and the evening examen to fade. Finish strong. Also, now that you've grow accustomed to praying ten Hail Marys per day, bump it up to a daily rosary for the final stretch.

DAY 24

MORTIFY YOUR FLESH

ODDS ARE, YOU can recall a moment when you've seen a toddler throwing a fit on the floor of a store because his parent wouldn't surrender to his demands for a particular toy or piece of candy. When a child is spoiled, it can't bear to hear the word "no." In the same respect, if we pamper ourselves with pleasure and saturate our senses with gratification, our bodies rebel when we withdraw such indulgences.

More often than not, the solution to this conflict is best addressed before the moment. In other words, if we expect our bodies to submit to the authority of our souls in a moment of great temptation, we would do well to train ourselves in advance by denying ourselves smaller pleasures.

For example, a country was once under attack from another nation, and the only way for the citizens to escape was by boat through frigid waters.

However, most of the boats were targeted by the enemy, and the refugees died of hypothermia in the water when their vessels sank. In order to flee to safety, one man began subjecting himself to freezing temperatures at home by submerging himself in ice-cold baths. He began with one-minute baths, and gradually extended his body's tolerance to the pain minute by minute. In time, he was able to withstand glacial temperatures for unusually long periods of time. When the day came for him to escape, his boat was sunk by the enemy and he alone was able to swim ashore to safety.

The mortification required of Christian men in today's culture is no different. Today, we will offer you two ways to mortify your senses, so that you will be well prepared to withstand the bombardments of the enemy.

ACTION

The root of the word "mortify" is the Latin *mors*, which means "death." From a Christian perspective, mortification is when we inflict small "deaths" to our desires in order to achieve a greater good. From a worldly perspective, these little deaths seem pointless and excessive. However, God brings life through them. Consider, for example, an example from nature: When a wildfire ravages a forest, it seems to leave only devastation behind. However, in order for the seeds of the lodgepole pine to sprout, a wildfire is required. Its pinecones sometimes wait for years, sealed by a layer of resin, until they are awakened by fire. After intense heat opens the seeds, a new stand of trees will thrive off the ashen, carbon-rich soil that the blaze created. In the same manner, a vibrant interior Christian life only emerges through mortification. Here are two ways you can do this at any time:

Mortify your flesh: We had mentioned this above, but it's worth repeating: Take a cold shower today. But don't endure the discomfort without offering it up for a specific intention. Offer it as a prayer for your future bride, for people trapped in the sex-trade industry, for women you have lusted after, or for all the men who will ever read this book.

Mortify your eyes: Although it's not in a man's power not to *see* seductive images, it's always within our power not to *look* at them. Temptations will inevitably come, but when you notice a woman jogging by, it isn't necessary to stare at her. If you see her, pray for her and keep your eyes

forward. Maintain custody of your eyes. St. Josemaría Escrivá asks, "Why look around if you carry
'your world' within you?"[38] Likewise, if an immodest scene appears on a screen, don't gawk it and
think, "Wow, I can't believe how evil the media
has become. Just look at the licentious images they
throw at us men! What an injustice. Just look at
her there." Quit buying yourself time to lust and
change the screen. With each temptation, improve
your reflex time. You're not averting your eyes
because her body is bad, but because God made her
too good to be degraded.

DAY 25

FAST

IN THE VISIBLE universe, there are laws of physics that govern creation, such as relativity, thermodynamics, motion, and so on. In a similar way, there are laws that exist within the invisible created universe. An example of this appears in the Gospel of Mark, when the disciples of Jesus perform an unsuccessful exorcism. The father of the possessed boy said to Jesus:

> Teacher, I brought my son to you, for he has a dumb spirit; and wherever it seizes him, it dashes him down; and he foams and grinds his teeth and becomes rigid; and I asked your disciples to cast it out, and they were not able.

Jesus asked that the boy be brought to Him, and when he was, the story continued:

[T]he spirit saw him, immediately it convulsed the boy, and he fell on the ground and rolled about, foaming at the mouth. . . . And when Jesus saw that a crowd came running together, he rebuked the unclean spirit, saying to it, "You dumb and deaf spirit, I command you, come out of him, and never enter him again." And after crying out and convulsing him terribly, it came out, and the boy was like a corpse; so that most of them said, "He is dead." But Jesus took him by the hand and lifted him up, and he arose. And when he had entered the house, his disciples asked him privately, "Why could we not cast it out?" And he said to them, "This kind cannot be driven out by anything but prayer and fasting." (Mark 9:17–29)

There is power in using our bodies to pray.

Beyond its intercessory power, fasting also trains us in self-mastery. It means denying things that would be fine for us to have, in order to strengthen us to resist things we shouldn't. Put it this way: If you can't say no to that cinnamon bun (the one that just came out of the oven and smells like happiness), how will you be able to say no to lust, which, it is safe to say, is far more alluring than the cinnamon bun.

Fasting does more than train you in self-mastery, though. Hunger pains offer a physical reminder to us that we're fasting, which raises our hearts and minds to God. Fasting is also a means of penance, purification, and preparation, as seen in many places throughout Scripture.[39] If Jesus Himself fasted and promised that His followers would do the same, we have no good reason to omit this form of prayer.[40]

ACTION

Next Friday, fast on bread and water if you're able. You might fast for twenty-four hours, or you might fast from sunrise to sunset, enabling you to have dinner once it's dark. A more moderate fast could involve skipping snacks between meals or drinking only water instead of other beverages. Throughout the day, make sacrifices on the spot. So even though you're "allowed" that second cup of coffee, choose not to have it. Though you could have dessert, don't. What is crucial about fasting is that you begin—that you stop thinking about it and actually do it! Right now, put down this book and consider what you will commit to fasting from. Be specific. Make this a weekly routine on Fridays, so that you're offering up some kind of penance to unite yourself to Christ's passion.

When you feel hunger pains, take this as a reminder from your body as to why you're making this sacrifice. Offer it as a prayer for something or someone specific, such as your future spouse. When you put a face on your fast, you add meaning to it. When it is done out of love, sacrifice becomes sweet.

DAY 26

READ SACRED BOOKS

MANY OF OUR problems with lust involve
images that have entered our imagination through
our eyes. It should not be surprising, then, that we
ought to use our eyes to purify our minds. One of
the best ways to do this is by means of holy reading.
As St. Josemaría Escrivá said, "Don't neglect your
spiritual reading. Reading has made many saints."[41]

In terms of which books to choose, we'll divide
them into three categories:

The first is the Word of God. Read Scripture daily.
A good place to begin is the four Gospels, as well as
the wisdom literature from the Old Testament, such
as the books of Proverbs, Sirach, and Wisdom.

The second category is writings from the saints
or books about their lives. Extraordinary amounts
of inspiration come from learning about individuals who lived extraordinary lives. Through learning about saints, you'll discover not only their

sanctity, but their humanity. You'll also establish holy friendships with them and will call upon their intercession more often when you know their lives and struggles.

The final category is books that offer you deeper moral and theological formation. For example, books on Theology of the Body, chastity, or any other topic of Church teaching that interests you. Always be reading a good book (or listen to the audio version of the book if it's available). When one ends, find another. If men today spent half the time reading holy books that they spend gaming, the world would be revolutionized. In the words of St. Athanasius, "You will not see anyone who is striving after his advancement who is not given to spiritual reading. And as to him who neglects it, the fact will soon be observed in his [lack of] progress."[42]

ACTION

In his thick Irish brogue accent, an elderly priest once said to me (Jason) in the confessional, "The word of God has power to drive out the evil one." For some reason, this phrase never left me. As I began to ponder what he meant by this, I realized that the Word of God was the weapon of choice used by Jesus when the devil tried to tempt Him in the wilderness.

Consider how Scripture counteracts the lies of the culture:

The world says, "You can't be expected to have self-control at your age, don't concern yourself with the example you set for your friends by your foul language and impurity." Scripture says, "Let no one despise your youth, but set the believers an example in speech and conduct, in love, in faith, in purity." (1 Tim 4:12)

A pornified culture says, "Your life is found in your hidden adventures online." Scripture says, "Your life is hid with Christ in God." (Col 3:3)

Lust says, "This is real life, that we would never be denied our every sexual desire, no matter how misogynistic or demeaning." Scripture says, "This is eternal life, that they know you, the only true God, and Jesus Christ whom you have sent." (John 17:3)

Also, instead of simplify reading from the Bible, memorize it and use it during moments of temptation. When tempting situations arrive, choose one of the short verses below and whisper it in prayer. Remember that this is not merely some mental exercise or religious distraction. The Word of God has power.

Blessed are the pure in heart, for they shall see God. (Matt 5:8)

The body is not meant for immorality, but for the Lord, and the Lord for the body. (1 Cor 6:13).

[W]hatever is true, whatever is honorable, whatever is just, whatever is pure, whatever is lovely, whatever is gracious, if there is any excellence, if there is anything worthy of praise, think about these things. (Phil 4:8)

He who loves purity of heart, and whose speech is gracious, will have the king as his friend. (Prov 22:11)

Create in me a clean heart, O God, and put a new and right spirit within me. (Ps 51:10)

[P]ut on the Lord Jesus Christ, and make no provision for the flesh, to gratify its desires. (Rom 13:14)

How can a young man keep his way pure? By guarding it according to thy word. (Ps 119:9)

DAY 27

PRACTICE SILENCE

THE QUALITY OF a man cannot be measured by his athletic ability, popularity, or success. Instead, the book of Sirach declares, "in his conversation is the test of a man" (Sirach 27:5 *NAB*). But why his speech? Consider how the following three saints answer that question:

The apostle James writes, "If anyone does not fall short in speech, he is a perfect man, able to bridle his whole body, also" (James 3:2).

We might be able to conceal many of our shortcomings, but as St. Basil the Great remarked, "Words are truly the images of the soul."[43]

But don't just fast from bad words or conversations. As St. Faustina said, "A talkative soul is empty inside."[44] The world isn't always in need of your opinion.

In order to develop the virtue of silence, focusing on what leaves our mouth is only half the task.

We also need to limit what enters our ears. We don't always need to be plugged into a source of external noise. Pope St. John Paul II noted that if you wish to encounter Christ "Above all, create silence in your interior. Let that ardent desire to see God arise from the depth of your hearts, a desire that at times is suffocated by the noise of the world and the seduction of pleasures."[45] As we learn to guard this silence, God will be more able to speak with us, moving our hearts to grow in love.

ACTION

Take a moment to meditate upon this brief passage from Father Anthony Paone, S.J., where Christ speaks to you about the need for silence in your life:

> My Child, there are times when you ought to keep to yourself and avoid conversation. There is no profit in unkind talk, rash talk, or indecent talk. What is the good of wasting time with idle disputes or with boasting?
>
> True, there are times when light conversation brings needed relief and necessary recreation, but talk which does not help the speaker or the

listener to lead a better life, is a shameful waste of precious time, time which will never return.

Think therefore before you speak, and you will never regret your words. The spoken word cannot be recalled. It is not always possible to undo the harm caused by thoughtless talk.

Many saints have avoided the company of men whenever possible to enjoy a closer union with Me. One of them once remarked: "As often as I have gone among men, I returned less of a man." Isn't this true of you when you talk too long? It is easier to keep silence altogether than to stop talking when you should.

In silence I shall speak to you with fewer interruptions. My words will come in the form of ideas, desires, intentions, and resolutions which arise within your soul. You will hear My voice with less distraction. Love silence and learn to use it well. Then you will draw closer to Me, as I am close to you.[46]

Take these words to heart and unplug from all noise today: No screens, no gaming, no social media, no music, no podcasts, and no idle talk. Only use your computer and phone for what's absolutely necessary for school and for work . . . and see what happens. This is not an optional exercise. We would ask that you not move on to Day 28 unless you follow through on this challenge. Not only is it essential to discover the fruit of pure silence, it's sobering to realize how attached we've all become to noise and distraction.

DAY 28

LISTEN TO HIM

THROUGHOUT THE Old Testament, God issues countless commands to mankind. However, did you know that God the Father only issues one in all of the pages of the New Testament? He commands, "This is my beloved Son, listen to him" (Mark 9:7).

For most men, the most difficult aspect of prayer is not carving out the time, speaking to God, praising Him, or interceding for others. The great challenge is sitting still and listening. We want to control situations, make an impact, and see results. Listening to God—and sometimes even to others—is not our thing. We're more comfortable with activity than receptivity. We prefer a posture of doing rather than letting it be done.

While this may be a strength for us in many areas of life, it's a major handicap when it comes to growing in our spirituality. We might even feel as if we're extremely active during our prayer time, but there could be a great deal of sloth at work because we only want to do what comes easiest. Therefore, step outside of your comfort zone, and "listen to him."

ACTION

Many men grow restless when they attempt to listen to God and hear nothing because they have never been taught how to pray. If you want to hear Him, here are three ways to make this happen:

First, don't wait until prayer time to create room for silence in your life. As we mentioned yesterday, unplug from noise throughout your day. You don't need to have a song, podcast, or video playing at every possible moment. If you create more space for quiet throughout your day, you're more likely to hear God's voice even when you're not praying!

Second, don't wait for an audible voice. More often than not, God "speaks" to us through promptings of the Holy Spirit that move our soul toward what is good. One priest said that the Holy Spirit speaks to us more than one hundred times per day. The question is whether or not we're listening.

Third, God wrote a book so that you would know exactly what He wants to say to you. Could you imagine standing before God in the next life, trying to explain why you found it so difficult to hear His voice when you never devoted time to read the Bible? When the thirty-three days of this program have ended, don't discontinue the practice of *Lectio Divina*. He will continue to speak to you through it.

The secret to a joyful life and a hope-filled future isn't about figuring out tomorrow; it's about listening to God today. God, the Author of Life, has something to say to you today. Therefore, carve out at least fifteen minutes of silent prayer per day.

DAY 29

REMEMBER YOUR GUARDIAN ANGEL

WHEN YOU THINK of a guardian angel, what comes to mind? Is it a feminine-looking feathered person in a nightgown escorting kids across a bridge? Or, how about a pudgy, winged toddler wrapped in a loincloth floating in the clouds? Unfortunately, it's fair to say that most Christian art is woefully inadequate in depicting the nature of angelic beings. Likewise, when the media portrays angels, they are depicted as having no other mission but to rescue people from physical harm. No mention is made of their role in guarding souls from spiritual ruin. However, this is the primary role of a guardian angel.

Angels are purely spiritual creatures who are servants and messengers of God. *The Catechism of the Catholic Church* adds, "They are personal and immortal creatures, surpassing in perfection all visible creatures, as the splendor of their glory bears witness."[47] The artistic renderings of angels, although imperfect, do convey deep truths. They are sometimes portrayed as feminine because they are beautiful. They are depicted as children because of their innocence. The wings represent their agility, and the clouds represent their heavenly origin. What's missing, though, is the fact that when angels appear in Scripture, they announce to those who see them "Do not be afraid!" because they are fearful to behold.

During the arrest of Jesus in the Garden of Gethsemane, Jesus tells Peter to sheathe his sword, reminding Peter that Jesus could easily call upon more than twelve legions of angels.[48] A Roman legion consisted of six thousand soldiers, which means that Jesus could have summoned seventy-two thousand angels. This would not have been unprecedented. In 2 Kings 6, a servant of the prophet Elisha panics upon seeing their city besieged by an army. Elisha reassures him, saying, "Fear not, for those who are with us are more than those who are with them." Then Elisha prayed to God that his eyes would see, and "the Lord opened the eyes of the young man, and he saw; and behold, the mountain was full of horses and chariots of fire round about

Elisha" (2 Kings 6:16–17). The mere sound of this army caused the enemies to "flee for their lives" in the night, leaving their belongings behind.[49]

In the same manner, Christians would do well to remember that although one might feel outnumbered in striving for virtue, the heavenly host surround us. As Jesus said to St. Faustina, "I will not delude you with prospects of peace and consolations; on the contrary, prepare for great battles. Know that you are now on a great stage where all heaven and earth are watching you. Fight like a knight, so that I can reward you. Do not be unduly fearful, because you are not alone."[50]

ACTION

Devotion to the holy angels is not an optional Christian devotion. Just as the angels ministered to Jesus after he was tempted in the desert by Satan and came to strengthen Him in His agony in the Garden of Gethsemane, they have been given to us to guard us on our way to heaven.

Therefore, take advantage of the intercessory power of your guardian angel, as well as the protection of St. Michael the Archangel or the healing graces of St. Raphael the Archangel. Here's how to seamlessly integrate these devotions into your daily life:

First, memorize the prayer to St. Michael the Archangel, and pray it when you feel tempted:

> Saint Michael the Archangel, defend us in battle. Be our protection against the wickedness and snares of the devil. May God rebuke him, we humbly pray; And do thou, O Prince of the Heavenly Host, by the power of God, cast into hell Satan and all the evil spirits who prowl about the world, seeking the ruin of souls.

A man once said to St. Padre Pio in confession, "But I am attached to my sins. For me they are a necessary way of life. Help me find a remedy." The saint gave him a prayer to St. Michael the Archangel and told him to pray it daily for four months![51]

Second, learn the Guardian Angel prayer, and add it to your morning routine: "Angel of God, my guardian dear, to whom God's love commits me here, ever this day be at my side, to light and guard, to rule and guide."

Also ask God for the grace to be more aware of your guardian angel. St. Josemaría Escrivá wrote,

"If you remembered the presence of your angel and the angels of your neighbors, you would avoid many of the foolish things which slip into your conversations."[52] Think about it: How could a man look at porn if he was aware of an angelic presence in the same room? How could a man fall into sin with his girlfriend while being conscious of both of their angels? Would a man lust after a woman in public if he knew her angel was watching the way he looked upon her? These are not mental tricks to avoid sin. These are exercises that unveil spiritual realities.

DAY 30

GO TO ST. JOSEPH

JUST AS MANY people have a difficult time connecting with the idea of angels because of the way they're often represented in Christian art, the same is true of St. Joseph for many men. Many artists, in an effort to safeguard the purity of the Virgin Mary, portray Joseph as an elderly man. This misses the mark for a number of reasons.

For one, there is no historical evidence that Joseph was an elderly man. Jewish men at the time of Christ would typically marry as soon as they could care for a family. For most men, this would be around eighteen years of age.

Second, God ordered Joseph to bring Mary from Nazareth to Bethlehem, to Egypt, and back to Nazareth. This arduous journey would have been several hundred miles. It would make no sense to ask an elderly man to undertake this dangerous voyage, let alone while guarding a teenage virgin and child.

Scripture indicates that Joseph was not a frail man. In Greek, the word for carpenter is *tekton*, which refers to a craftsman who works with heavy materials. The book of Isaiah speaks of carpenters as men who would cut down cedars.[53] They would hew their own lumber, carry the beams to their workshops, and craft it into doorway lintels, yoke for oxen, and other things. As any father trains a son, St. Joseph would have trained Jesus how to carry these beams through the streets of the Holy Land.

Third, men do not automatically progress in purity as they grow older. Recall the story of Susanna from the book of Daniel. She was a beautiful and righteous woman, but "two elders used to see her every day, going in and walking about, and they began to desire her. And they perverted their minds and turned away their eyes from looking to Heaven or remembering righteous judgments." When they trapped her and attempted to seduce her, she rejected their advances. To escape their crime, the pair lied and accused her of infidelity. She was brought to judgment and further degraded, as Scripture tell us: "As she was veiled, the wicked men ordered her to be unveiled, that they might feed upon her beauty." Daniel, inspired by the Holy Spirit, interrupts the false trial, separates the men, and exposes their plot. To one, he said, "How you have grown evil with age!" and to the other, "Offspring of Canaan, not of Judah . . . beauty has seduced you, lust has perverted your heart" (Dan 13). The two were executed, Susanna's honor was restored, and the people revered Daniel for his wisdom.

In this moving narrative, Daniel did not partake in the degradation of Susanna. He used his youthful vigor to defend her dignity when she was unable to do so. In the same manner, God endowed Joseph with youthful purity to guard the innocence of Mary. For good reason, the Church honors him in the Litany of St. Joseph as the Guardian of the Virgin and the Terror of Demons.

ACTION

The information above makes a case for the youthfulness of St. Joseph. But now ponder what this means: In His eternal wisdom, God the Father entrusted the spotless purity and Immaculate Heart of the Blessed Virgin Mary . . . to a college-aged man! Why would God do this? Because no man on earth was more fit for this task than Joseph.

Compelled by a misguided sense of piety, some people are afraid to think about Joseph's love for Mary, and hers for him. But let us recall they were already engaged when the angel Gabriel appeared to Mary. The two were anticipating married life together. It is safe to say that Joseph was in love with her. How could he not be? She was Mary! However, his love was not a threat to her purity. In fact, it was precisely his love for her that safeguarded her purity! Her virginity was not protected by an old man's senility or sterility, but by Joseph's virtue and virility.

Meditate on this love. Contemplate how a young, strong Joseph would have treated Our Lady with tremendous reverence. Don't be afraid to imagine his pure affection toward her. Living in today's culture, our imaginations are easily polluted by images of lust. For this reason, we need to cleanse our imagination by means of prayerful contemplation. Ruminate on these things, and then when you feel tempted, call upon the aid of St. Joseph, Terror of Demons and Guardian of the Virgin.

DAY 31

BEHOLD YOUR MOTHER

WOMEN HAVE A curious power to bring out the best and the worst in us. I (Jason) recall being at a bookstore and seeing four high school boys huddled around a smutty magazine. A beautiful and athletic twenty-something-year-old woman walked over and began reading a magazine right next to them. At the sight of her, one guy coughed, another dropped the magazine back on the rack, and they all bolted out the door—as if they'd become spontaneously disinterested in half-naked women.

What happened? My theory is this: Few things inspire masculinity in a man more than the presence of true femininity. While it is essential as a Christian to have a personal relationship with Christ, Our Lord also wants us to know and love His mother. In fact, when a man takes up a devotion to Our Lady and entrusts himself to her, her femininity begins to inspire his masculinity as he seeks to become worthy of her. Perhaps this is one reason why Bishop Hugh Doyle once wrote that "No one can live continually in sin and continue to say the Rosary: either they will give up sin or they will give up the Rosary."[54]

Consider how earnestly the saints encouraged us to draw near to her. St. Louis de Montfort, who was one of the greatest apostles of Marian devotion, exclaimed:

> The formation and the education of the great saints who will come at the end of the world are reserved for her. . . . When the Holy Ghost, her Spouse, has found Mary in a soul, He flies there. He enters there in His fullness; He communicates Himself to that soul abundantly, and to the full extent to which it makes room for His spouse (Mary). . . . [The devils] fear one of her sighs for a soul more than the prayers of all the saints, and one of her threats against them more than all other torments. . . . We make more progress is a brief period of submission to and dependence on Mary, than in whole years of following our own will and of relying upon ourselves. . . . This good Mother and powerful Princess of the Heavens would rather dispatch

battalions of millions of angels to assist one of her servants than that it should ever be said that a faithful servant of Mary, who trusted in her, had had to succumb to the malice, the number, and the vehemence of his enemies.[55]

Heed his advice and hold nothing back from her. In prayer, ask her to teach you how to look at women. Ask her how she would have you treat her daughters.

ACTION

At the beginning of our thirty-three-day journey, we encouraged you to carry a rosary with you at all times. If you've been faithful to this small devotion, what effects have you seen from it?

Second, have you made the time for a daily rosary? While some people disregard the rosary, considering it a pious devotional of Catholic grandmothers, St. Padre Pio remarked, "Some people are so foolish that they think they can go through life without the help of the Blessed Mother. Love the Madonna and pray the Rosary, for her Rosary is the weapon against the evils of the world today."[56]

Finally, do not merely pray the rosary. Promote it! If you think you're unfit to do so, consider the life of Blessed Bartolo Longo. He was raised in a devout Catholic home but fell away from the faith in college. He began dabbling in the occult, participating in seances, practicing sexual promiscuity, and even became a satanic priest! Afflicted with suicidal thoughts and tormented by diabolical visions, he was guided by a priest to amend his life and Bartolo dedicated himself to promoting the rosary. In 1980, thirty thousand people gathered at his beatification ceremony, as Pope St. John Paul II declared him to be "The Apostle of the Rosary." Nothing from your past can disqualify you from leading others to God through Our Lady.

DAY 32

BE INTENSELY EUCHARISTIC

ACCORDING TO THE market research firm Nielsen, the average person spends eleven hours and six minutes per day interacting with a screen, whether it be a phone, computer, or television (which, interestingly, adds up to 666 minutes).[57] If that's not enough of a wake-up call, do the math and it adds up to more than thirty-six years of one's lifetime! Odds are, this time could be spent more productively. When a man lies on his deathbed, the one thing he'll never wish is that he could have had more screen time.

Granted, technology can be a great blessing in our lives. But what if we redirected only a fraction of our screen time to Eucharistic Adoration? Instead of binge-watching one more show, what if we gave thirty minutes of our day to attending a daily Mass? A seismic shift would happen in our lives.

When Moses descended from Mount Sinai after speaking with God, his face had become so radiant that he needed to wear a veil in the presence of the Israelites.[58] In the same manner, when men live intensely Eucharistic lives, God works in and through them in a wondrous and undeniable manner. We may think that we could do more good for God through our activity, but St. John of the Cross reminds us:

> Let those, then, who are singularly active, who think they can win the world with their preaching and exterior works, observe here that they would profit the Church and please God much more, not to mention the good example they would give, were they to spend at least half of this time with God in prayer. . . . They would then certainly accomplish more, and with less labor, by one work than they otherwise would by a thousand. For through their prayer they would merit this result, and themselves be spiritually strengthened. Without prayer they would do a great deal of hammering but accomplish little, and sometimes nothing, and even at times cause harm. . . . However much they may appear to achieve externally, they will in substance be accomplishing

nothing; it is beyond doubt that good works can be performed only by the power of God.[59]

Not only does time spent in prayer make us more effective apostles, Eucharistic Adoration is particularly efficacious in battling sins of the flesh for our own sakes. For one, our eyes have looked upon so much that is impure that we are deeply in need of seeing what is holy. Second, the Eucharistic language of "This is my body, given up for you" inverts the language of lust, which says, "This is your body, taken by me." As men, our call to love is not only stamped into our bodies, but also into the very Body of Christ in the Eucharist. Just as a husband gives himself to his bride, in order that she may bear life, Christ the bridegroom gives His body to His bride, the Church, so that we might have eternal life. This is not sexualizing the Eucharist. This is realizing the sacredness of our sexuality. It makes visible the invisible love of God!

Consider this remarkable quote from Pope St. John Paul II:

Jesus speaks to us in the wonderful language of the gift of self and of love so great as to give our own life for it. Is that an easy thing? You know very well that it is not! It is not easy to forget our self, but if we do, it draws us away from possessive and narcissistic love and opens us up to the joy of a love that is self-giving. This Eucharistic school of freedom and charity teaches us to overcome superficial emotions in order to be rooted firmly in what is true and good; it frees us from self-attachment in order to open ourselves to others. It teaches us to make the transition from an *affective* love to an *effective* love. For love is not merely a feeling; it is an act of will that consists of preferring, in a constant manner, the good of others to the good of oneself: "Greater love has no man than this, that a man lays down his life for his friends."

Therefore, if you desire freedom, spend generous amounts of time sitting in the school of the Eucharist. There, you will discover what it means to give up your body for your bride.

ACTION

Odds are, there is a Catholic Church not far from you. Today or tomorrow, make a visit to the Blessed

Sacrament as you conclude this thirty-three-day journey. If you can carve out the time to attend a Mass and receive Holy Communion, even better. After receiving the Eucharist or while spending time in adoration, offer the following prayers:

Dearest Jesus! I know well that every perfect gift, and above all others that of chastity, depends upon the most powerful assistance of thy Providence and that without thee a creature can do nothing. Therefore, I pray thee to defend, with thy grace, chastity and purity in my soul as well as in my body. And if I have ever received through my senses any impression that could stain my chastity and purity, do thou, who art the supreme Lord of all my powers, take it from me, that I may with an immaculate heart advance in thy love and service, offering myself chaste all the days of my life on the most pure altar of thy divinity. Amen.

O immaculate heart of Mary, Virgin most pure, mindful of the terrible moral dangers threatening on all sides and aware of my own human weakness, I voluntarily place myself, body, and soul, this day and always, under your loving maternal care and protection. I consecrate to you my body with all its members, asking you to help me never to use it as an occasion of sin to others. Help me to remember that my body is "the temple of the Holy Ghost" and use it according to God's holy will for my own salvation and the salvation of others. I consecrate to you my soul, asking you to watch over it, and to bring it home safe to you and to Jesus in heaven for all eternity. O Mary, my Mother, all that I am, all that I have is yours. Keep me and guard me as your property and possession. Amen.

DAY 33

LIVE IN FREEDOM

IN THE LATE 1800s in China, a young husband and father named Mark Ji Tianxiang fell ill with a severe stomach illness. Because he was also a physician, he was able to treat himself with a common pain medicine at the time, opium. Although the illness passed, a drug addiction remained in its place. Mark went to the sacrament of reconciliation, confessed his sins, and soon fell back into them. Again, he returned to confession, only to regress back into his addiction, despite the great societal shame associated with it. After repeating this cycle for years, his priest asked him to no longer return to confession until he had broken free from the grasp of his addiction (which, obviously, isn't the best pastoral advice).

Mark heeded his counsel and continued his struggle without the grace of the sacraments. He continued to attend Mass, but also did not receive Holy Communion. For thirty years, he battled his addiction while praying that God would make him a martyr. In the year 1900, when Mark was sixty-six years old and still addicted to opium, God answered his prayer. The Boxer Rebellion swept through China and tens of thousands of Christians were massacred. Mark, along with nine members of his family were dragged off to prison where they awaited their execution. On their way, Mark's grandson fearfully asked him, "Grandpa, where are we going?" Mark replied, "We're going home."

One by one, the torturers began beheading his six grandchildren, his two daughters-in-law, and his son. Mark begged the executioners to kill him last, so that none of his family members would have to die alone. At last, Mark went to his death singing the Litany of the Blessed Virgin Mary. He is now a canonized saint in the Catholic Church . . . who died addicted to opium! St. Mark Ji Tianxiang is proof that the saint is not the one who does not have a mess in his life. The saint is the one who gives his mess entirely to Jesus Christ.

While this might seem to be a somber conclusion to our thirty-three-day journey, we have saved this story for last because no matter where you stand today, you belong entirely to God. As we said at the beginning, you are loved, and God will complete the good work He has begun in you (Phil 1:6). Rest in this promise.

ACTION

In the past several weeks, we've presented every strategy and weapon imaginable to overcome lust and help you grow in freedom. Now, it's up to you to use them. Although there won't be a specific action waiting for you to accomplish tomorrow, you'll find that there will be a time and place for each of the things you've learned.

Not long from now, you will be tempted. When that moment comes, we invite you pause. Recall the graces you've received during this time and select a weapon from your arsenal. Will you thank God for her beauty and pray for her? Will you identify the trigger or root that might be exaggerating the allure of this temptation? Will you turn to St. Joseph, your guardian angel, or an accountability partner for strength? No matter what your decision may be, always know that this isn't just an opportunity to fall. This is an invitation to love in imitation of Christ, who gave His up body for His bride. Now go do the same.

FORGED TO FIGHT

FIGHT CLUB

ALTHOUGH THESE thirty-three days have come to an end, chastity is a lifelong commitment to follow Christ, to fight for our brides, and to combat with brother warriors. Therefore, we invite you to continue in fellowship to purify your eyes, imagination, and actions.

One of the best ways to do this is to create a Fight Club. Fight Club Catholic is a brotherhood of men committed to purifying their hearts in order to see God in women, in themselves, and ultimately in heaven. Members understand that the battle isn't merely about breaking free from unwanted sexual behavior. Rather, the focus is upon the words of Christ: "Blessed are the pure of heart for they shall see God" (Matt 5:8). Purity enables a man to encounter Christ and discover the mission to which he is called.

Fight Club Catholic members fight for *God*, for *her* (their future brides or the Church, and their sisters in humanity), and for *each other*. To learn how to establish a Fight Club, go to fightclubcatholic.com.

Listen to **Jason** and **Matt's Podcasts!**

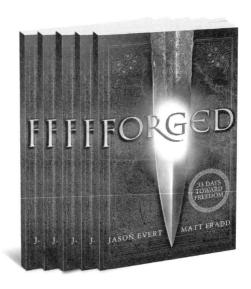

Share *FORGED* with others for as little as $3 per copy

Think of the men in your community who could benefit from reading it:

- Start a book study in your college dorm
- Give it away in your youth or young adult group
- Share copies with your Confirmation or religious ed classes
- Study it in your high school religion class
- Distribute copies on retreats
- Offer it as a gift for graduations and birthdays
- Donate copies to your campus ministry program

To order, visit: Chastity.com

GOT QUESTIONS? GET ANSWERS.

WATCH VIDEOS
GET RELATIONSHIP ADVICE
LAUNCH A PROJECT
READ ANSWERS TO TOUGH QUESTIONS
FIND HELP TO HEAL FROM THE PAST
LISTEN TO POWERFUL TESTIMONIES
SHOP FOR GREAT RESOURCES
SCHEDULE A SPEAKER

ENDNOTES

1 Summa II.II. 138.

2 C. S. Lewis, *The Weight of Glory* (New York: Harper Collins, 1949), 26.

3 C. S. Lewis, *Mere Christianity* (New York: Harper Collins, 1952), 49.

4 Bruce Marshall, *The World, The Flesh, and Father Smith* (Boston: Houghton Mifflin Company, 1945), 108.

5 Josemaría Escrivá, *The Way* (New York: Scepter, 2002), 42.

6 Escrivá, *The Way*, 43.

7 Escrivá, *The Way*, 21.

8 Brother Michael Dimond, *Padre Pio* (Fillmore, NY: Most Holy Family Monastery, 2006), 52.

9 Joseph Cardinal Ratzinger, *God and the World* (San Francisco: Ignatius Press, 2002), 44.

10 R. M. Bergner and A. J. Bridges, "The Significance of Heavy Pornography Involvement for Romantic Partners: Research and Clinical Implications," *Journal of Sex and Marital Therapy* 28 (2002): 193–206.

11 "Emily," in Henry J. Rogers, *The Silent War: Ministering to Those Caught in the Deception of Pornography* (Green Forest, AR: New Leaf Press, 2007).

12 Jason Evert and Crystalina Evert, *How to Find Your Soulmate Without Losing Your Soul* (San Diego, CA: Totus Tuus Press, 2011), 25–26.

13 Saint Augustine; Paul Thigpen, *A Dictionary of Quotes from the Saints* (North Carolina: Tan Books, 2001), 101.

14 Jay Stringer, *Unwanted* (Colorado Springs: NavPress, 2018), 9.

15 Stringer, *Unwanted*, 60.

16 Stringer, *Unwanted*, 60.

17 Michael John Cusick, *Surfing for God* (Nashville, Thomas Nelson: 2012), 95.

18 Johann Hari, *Chasing the Scream* (New York, Bloomsbury: 2015), 293.

19 St. Philip Neri, in Saint Alphonsus Liguori, *The Practice of the Love of Jesus Christ* (New York: Aeterna Press, 2016).

20 Matt. 10:8.

21 Alex Woodie, "Today's Baseball Analytics Make Moneyball Look Like Child's Play," Datanami.com, October 24, 2014.

22 Father Jacques Philippe, *Searching For and Maintaining Peace* (New York: Society of Saint Paul, 2002).

23 St. Padre Pio, in James Kubicki, *A Year of Daily Offerings* (Notre Dame, IN: Ave Maria Press, 2016), 335.

24 *The Saint of Silence and the Message of Our Lady*, 18–20.

25 St. John Bosco, in Paul Thigpen, *A Dictionary of Quotes from the Saints* (Ann Arbor, MI: Charis Books, 2001), 124.

26 St. Gregory the Great, in Venerable Louis of Granada, OP, *The Sinner's Guide* (New York: Aeterna Press, 2015), 202.

27 C. S. Lewis, *The Screwtape Letters* (New York, Harper Collins: 2013), 53.

28 Matt 4; Luke 4.

29 Julia C. Basso and Wendy A. Suzuki, "The Effects of Acute Exercise on Mood, Cognition, Neurophysiology, and Neurochemical Pathways: A Review," *Brain Plasticity* 2:2 (2017): 127–152.

30 St. Leo the Great, in Francis W. Johnston, *Voice of the Saints* (Gastonia, NC: Tan Books, 1986).

31 St. Ephraem, in Thigpen, *A Dictionary of Quotes from the Saints*, 228.

32 Rev. Daniel R. Jennings, M.A., "The Average Life Expectancy of a Porn Star," http://danielrjennings.org/TheAverageLifeExpectancyOfAPornStar.html.

33 Dr. Mary Anne Layden, "The Science Behind Pornography Addiction," 18 Nov. 2004. Reported in U.S Senate Hearings: *U. S. Senate Committee on Commerce, Science & Transportation*. Web. 24 Nov. 2009.

34 Karol Wojtyła, *Love and Responsibility* (New York: Farrar, Straus and Giroux, 1981), 131.

35 Linda Lovelace, in Fred Strebeigh, "Defining Law on the Feminist Frontier," *New York Times*, October 6, 1991.

36 Mike Tyson interview with Jeremy Schapp, *E:60*, ESPN, July 20, 2017.

37 Oliver Berton et al., "Essential Role of BDNF in Mesolimbic Dopamine Pathway in Social Defeat Stress," *Science* 311 (February 2006), 864–68; Joe S. McIlhaney Jr. and Freda McKissic Bush, *Hooked* (Chicago: Northfield Publishing, 2008), 85.

38 Escrivá, *The Way*, 50.

39 Dan 10:1–3; Deut 9; Matt 4:1–2.

40 Luke 5:35.

41 Escrivá, *The Way*, 39.

42 Thomas Morrow, *Who's Who in Heaven* (Steubenville, OH: Emmaus Road Publishing, 2012), xi.

43 Rosemary Guiley, *The Quotable Saint* (New York: Visionary Living, Inc., 2002), 304.

44 St. Maria Faustina Kowalska, *Diary: Divine Mercy in My Soul* (Stockbridge, MA: Marians of the Immaculate

Conception, 2002), 118.

45 Pope John Paul II, "Message for 2004 World Youth Day,"
    Vatican City, March 1, 2004.

46 Anthony Paone, S.J., *My Daily Bread* (New York:
    Confraternity of the Precious Blood, 1954).

47 *Catechism of the Catholic Church* 2339 (San Francisco:
    Ignatius Press, 1994), 333.

48 Matt 26:53.

49 2 Kings 7:6–7.

50 St. Maria Faustina, *Diary*, 1760.

51 Dorothy Gaudiose, *Prophet of the People* (New York: Society
    of Saint Paul, 2018), 248.

52 Guiley, *The Quotable Saint*, 8.

53 Cf. Is 44:14.

54 Bishop Hugh Doyle, in "The Rosary," ewtn.com.

55 St. Louis de Montfort, *True Devotion to Mary* (Rockford, IL:
    Tan Books, 1985), 21, 31, 98, 133.

56 Diane and Deacon Ron Allen, "Pray, Hope, and Don't
    Worry," *Padre Pio Newsletter*, 75:3.

57 Nielsen Total Audience Report, 2018.

58 Cf. Exodus 34.

59 St. John of the Cross, *The Collected Works of Saint John of
    the Cross* (Washington DC: ICS Publications, 2017), 588.